300 FANTASTIC FACTS

SPACE

300 FANTASTIC FACTS

SPACE

Written by: Sue Becklake, Steve Parker

Miles Kelly

First published in 2015 by Miles Kelly Publishing Ltd
Harding's Barn, Bardfield End Green, Thaxted, Essex, CM6 3PX, UK

2 4 6 8 10 9 7 5 3 1

Publishing Director Belinda Gallagher
Creative Director Jo Cowan
Designers Rob Hale, Andrea Slane
Cover Designer Rob Hale
Editorial Assistant Meghan Oosterhuis
Image Manager Liberty Newton
Production Manager Elizabeth Collins
Reprographics Stephan Davis, Jennifer Cozens, Thom Allaway
Consultants Sue Becklake, Steve Parker, Clint Twist
Indexer Jane Parker

ISBN 978-1-78209-737-2

Printed in China

British Library Cataloguing-in-Publication Data
A catalogue record for this book is available from the British Library

Made with paper from a sustainable forest

www.mileskelly.net
info@mileskelly.net

Contents

1 Space is all around Earth, high
above the air. Here on Earth we are
surrounded by air. If you go upwards –
for example, by climbing a high mountain
or flying in a plane – the air grows thinner
until there is none at all. Space officially
begins 100 kilometres up from sea level.
It is mostly empty, but there are many
exciting things such as planets, stars and
galaxies. People who travel in space are
called astronauts.

▶ In space, astronauts wear
spacesuits to go outside a space
station or a spacecraft as it
circles Earth. Much farther away
are planets, stars and galaxies.

Our life-giving star

2 **The Sun is our nearest star.** Most stars are so far away they look like points of light in the sky, but the Sun looks different because it is much closer to us. The Sun is not solid, like Earth. It is a huge ball of super-hot gases, so hot that they glow like the flames of a bonfire.

◀ The Sun's hot, glowing gas is always on the move, bubbling up to the surface and sinking back down again.

3 **Nothing could live on Earth without the Sun.** Deep in its centre the Sun is constantly making energy that keeps its gases hot and glowing. This energy works its way to the surface where it escapes as heat and light. Without it, Earth would be cold and dark with no life at all.

PROMINENCE

Solar prominences can reach temperatures of 10,000°C.

SOLAR FLARE

Solar flares erupt in a few minutes, then take more than half an hour to die away again.

SUNSPOT

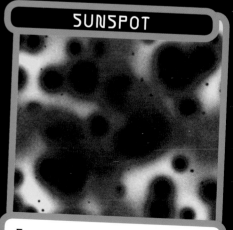

Groups of sunspots seem to move across the Sun over two weeks, as the Sun rotates.

4 The Sun is often spotty. Sunspots appear on the surface, some wider than Earth. They look dark because they are cooler than the rest of the Sun. Solar flares – explosions of energy – can suddenly shoot out from the Sun. The Sun also throws huge loops of gas called prominences out into space.

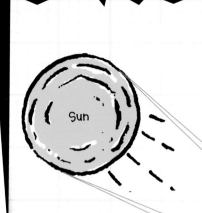

▶ When the Moon casts a shadow on Earth, there is a solar eclipse.

Sun

Moon

Earth

Total eclipse

5 When the Moon hides the Sun there is a solar eclipse. Every so often, the Sun, Moon and Earth line up in space so that the Moon comes directly between the Earth and the Sun. This stops the sunlight from reaching a small area on Earth. This area grows dark and cold, as if night has come early.

▲ A photo of a solar eclipse on 1 August 2008 shows the Moon totally blocking the Sun, and reveals the Sun's halo–like corona – part of its atmosphere not normally seen because the Sun's surface is too bright.

I DON'T BELIEVE IT!
The surface of the Sun is nearly 60 times hotter than boiling water. It is so hot it would melt a spacecraft flying near it.

WARNING
Never look directly at the Sun, especially not through a telescope or binoculars. It is so bright it will harm your eyes and could even make you blind.

A family of planets

6 The Sun is surrounded by a family of circling planets called the Solar System. This family is held together by an invisible force called gravity, which pulls things towards each other. It is the same force that pulls us down to the ground and stops us from floating away. The Sun's gravity pulls on the planets and keeps them circling around it.

I DON'T BELIEVE IT!
If the Sun was the size of a large beach ball, Earth would be as small as a pea, and the Moon would look like a pinhead.

JUPITER

VENUS

EARTH

MERCURY

SUN

7 Earth is one of eight planets in the Sun's family. They all circle the Sun at different distances from it. The four planets nearest to the Sun are all balls of rock. The other four planets are much bigger and are made of gas and liquid.

▼ The eight planets are all different. Mercury, nearest the Sun, is small and hot. Then Venus, Earth and Mars are rocky and cooler. Beyond them Jupiter, Saturn, Uranus and Neptune are large and cold.

NEPTUNE

URANUS

SATURN

8 Moons circle the planets, travelling with them round the Sun. Earth has one moon. It circles Earth while Earth circles round the Sun. Mars has two tiny moons, but Mercury and Venus have none at all. There are large families of moons, like miniature solar systems, around all the large gas planets.

9 There are millions of smaller members in the Sun's family. Some are tiny specks of dust speeding through space between the planets. Larger chunks of rock, many as large as mountains, are called asteroids. Comets come from the edge of the Solar System, skimming past the Sun before they disappear again.

Planet of life

Location of Earth

10 **The planet we live on is called Earth.** It is a round ball of rock. On the outside (where we live) the rock is hard and solid. But deep below our feet, inside the Earth, the rock is hot enough to melt. You can sometimes see this hot rock showering out of an erupting volcano.

Inner core

Outer core

Mantle

Crust

Atmosphere

▶ Earth's inner core is made of iron. It is very hot and keeps the outer core as liquid. Outside this is the mantle, made of thick rock. The thin surface layer that we live on is called the crust.

▼ No other planet in the Solar System has liquid water on its surface, so Earth is the only known planet suitable for life.

11 **Earth is the only planet with life.** From space, Earth is a blue-and-white planet, with huge oceans and wet masses of cloud. Animals – including people – and plants can live on Earth because of all this water.

12 **Sunshine gives us daylight when it is night on the other side of the Earth.** When it is daytime, your part of the Earth faces towards the Sun and it is light. At night, your part faces away from the Sun and it is dark. Day follows night because the Earth is always turning.

As Earth rotates, the day and night halves shift gradually around the world. Earth turns eastwards, so the Sun rises in the east as each part of the world spins to face it.

I DON'T BELIEVE IT!
The Moon has no air. When astronauts went to the Moon they had to take air with them in their spacecraft and spacesuits.

13 **Craters on the Moon are scars from space rocks crashing into the surface.** When a rock smashes into the Moon at high speed, it leaves a saucer-shaped dent, pushing some of the rock outwards into a ring of mountains.

14 **Look for the Moon on clear nights and watch how it seems to change shape.** Over a month it changes from a thin crescent to a round shape. This is because sunlight is reflected by the Moon. We see the full Moon when the sunlit side faces Earth and a thin, crescent shape when most of the sunlit side is facing away from us.

Crescent moon

Half moon

Full moon

Half moon

Crescent moon

▲ During the first half of each monthly cycle, the Moon waxes (appears to grow). During the second half, it wanes (dwindles) back to a crescent-shape.

▲ Dark patches are called seas although there is no water on the Moon.

The Earth's neighbours

15 Venus and Mars are the nearest planets to Earth. Venus is closer to the Sun than Earth while Mars is farther away. Each takes a different amount of time to circle the Sun and we call this its year. A year on Venus is 225 days, on Earth 365 days and on Mars 687 days.

16 Venus is the hottest planet, even though Mercury is closer to the Sun. Heat builds up on Venus because it is completely covered by clouds that trap the heat, like the glass in a greenhouse.

▲ Dense clouds surround Venus, making it difficult to observe, so the Magellan spacecraft spent four years mapping the surface with radar (bouncing radio waves) to produce images like this.

▲ Under its clouds, Venus has hundreds of volcanoes, large and small, all over its surface. We do not know if any of them are still erupting.

17 The clouds around Venus are poisonous — they contain drops of acid that would burn your skin. They are not like clouds on Earth, which are made of droplets of water. They are thick, and do not let much sunshine reach the surface of Venus.

Location of Mars

18
Winds on Mars whip up huge dust storms that can cover the whole planet. Mars is very dry, like a desert, and covered in red dust. When a space probe called *Mariner 9* arrived there in 1971, the whole planet was hidden by dust clouds.

Solar panel

Camera

Radio aerial

▲ *Mariner 9* was the first space probe to circle another planet. Since that time more than 30 other crafts have travelled there and several have soft-landed.

19
Mars has the largest volcano in the Solar System. It is called Olympus Mons and is three times as high as Mount Everest, the tallest mountain on Earth. Olympus Mons is an old volcano and it has not erupted for millions of years.

LIFE ON MARS
Mars is the best known planet besides Earth. It is dry, rocky and covered in dust. Look in books and on the Internet to find out more about Mars. What do you think it would be like to live there?

20
There are plans to send astronauts to Mars but the journey would take six months or more. The astronauts would have to take with them everything they need for the journey there and back and for their stay on Mars.

◄ The Hubble Space Telescope has captured a giant dust storm in this picture of Mars. The bright orange patch in the middle shows where the dry red dust is blown up by strong winds.

The smallest of all

21 Mercury looks like our Moon. It is a round, cratered ball of rock. Although a little larger than the Moon, like the Moon it has no air.

MAKE CRATERS

You will need:
flour   baking tray
a marble or a stone

1. Spread some flour about 2 centimetres deep on a baking tray and smooth over the surface.
2. Drop a marble or a small round stone onto the flour.
3. Can you see the saucer-shaped crater the marble makes?

◀ Mercury has high cliffs and long ridges as well as craters. Astronomers think it cooled and shrank in the past, making its surface wrinkled.

CRATERS

Mercury's many craters show how often it was hit by space rocks. One was so large that it shattered rocks on the other side of the planet.

22 The sunny side of Mercury is boiling hot but the night side is freezing cold. Being the nearest planet to the Sun, the sunny side can get twice as hot as an oven. But Mercury spins round slowly so the night side has time to cool down, and there is no air to trap the heat. The night side becomes more than twice as cold as Antarctica – the coldest place on Earth.

Location of dwarf planets

23 Tiny, rocky Pluto was discovered in 1930. At first it was called a planet, but in 2006, it was re-classified as a dwarf planet. It is less than half the width of Mercury. In fact, Pluto is smaller than our Moon.

25 Aside from Pluto, four other dwarf planets have been named. They are called Ceres, Eris, Makemake and Haumea (in order from the closest to the Sun to the farthest away). Eris is larger than Pluto.

ERIS

PLUTO

CERES

▲ Ceres orbits between Mars and Jupiter. Pluto orbits further away from the Sun than Neptune, and Eris is further out still.

24 If you stood on the surface of Pluto, the Sun would not look much brighter than any other stars. Pluto is so far from the Sun that it receives little heat and is completely covered in ice.

26 The first space probe to visit Pluto will be *New Horizons*. It blasted off in 2006 and is due to reach the dwarf planet by 2015. If all goes well it will then carry on to the outer region of the Solar System, called the Kuiper Belt.

The biggest of all

27 Jupiter is more massive than the other seven planets in the Solar System put together. It is 11 times as wide as Earth, although it is still much smaller than the Sun. Saturn, the next largest planet, is more than nine times as wide as the Earth.

28 Jupiter has more than 60 moons. Its moon Io has many active volcanoes that throw out huge plumes of material, making red blotches and dark marks on its orange-yellow surface.

29 The Great Red Spot on Jupiter is a 300-year-old storm. It was first noticed about 300 years ago and is at least twice as wide as the Earth. It rises above the rest of the clouds and swirls around like storm clouds on Earth.

◀ Jupiter's fast winds blow clouds into coloured bands around the planet.

▼ There are many storms on Jupiter but none are as large or long-lasting as the Great Red Spot.

Io

Europa

Ganymede

Callisto

These four large moons were discovered by Galileo Galilei in 1610, which is why they are known as the Galilean moons.

Location of Saturn

▶ Although Saturn's rings are very wide, they stretch out in a very thin layer around the planet.

30 The shining rings around Saturn are made of millions of chunks of ice. These circle the planet like tiny moons and shine by reflecting sunlight from their surfaces. Some are as small as ice cubes while others are as large as a car.

31 Jupiter and Saturn are gas giants. They have no solid surface for a spacecraft to land on. All that you can see are the tops of their clouds. Beneath the clouds, the planets are made mostly of gas (like air) and liquid (water is a liquid).

▼ Taken with the Hubble Space Telescope, this image shows a detailed view of Saturn's southern hemisphere and its rings.

I DON'T BELIEVE IT!
For its size, Saturn is lighter than any other planet. If there was a large enough sea, it would float like a cork.

32 Jupiter and Saturn spin round so fast that they bulge out in the middle. This can happen because they are not made of solid rock. As they spin, their clouds are stretched out into light and dark bands around them.

So far away

This photo shows an aurora display (the glowing blue dot) on Uranus. Aurorae are made by tiny particles given off by the Sun, known as the solar wind. These get trapped by a planet's magnetism and start to glow.

33 **Uranus and Neptune are gas giants like Jupiter and Saturn.** They are the next two planets beyond Saturn but are much smaller, being less than half as wide. They too have no hard surface. Their cloud tops make Uranus and Neptune both look blue. They are very cold, being so far from the Sun.

► Uranus's moon Miranda looks as though it has been split apart and put back together again.

34 **Uranus seems to 'roll' around the Sun.** Most of the other planets spin upright like tops, but Uranus spins on its side. It may have been knocked over when something crashed into it millions of years ago.

▼ Uranus's five largest moons are big enough to be classified as dwarf planets, but they are not in direct orbit of the Sun.

	Name	Diameter	Year of discovery
1	Titania	1578 km	1787
2	Oberon	1523 km	1787
3	Umbriel	1169 km	1851
4	Ariel	1158 km	1851
5	Miranda	472 km	1948

35 **Uranus has more than 25 moons, and there are probably more to be discovered.** Most are very small, but Titania, the largest, is 1578 kilometres across, which makes it the eighth largest moon in the Solar System.

Location of Neptune

36
Neptune had a storm that disappeared. When the *Voyager 2* space probe flew past Neptune in 1989 it spotted a huge storm, like a dark version of the Great Red Spot on Jupiter. But when the Hubble Space Telescope looked at Neptune in 1994, the storm had gone.

▲ *Voyager 2* is the only probe to visit Neptune and send back close up pictures of the planet.

37
Neptune has bright blue clouds that make the whole planet look blue. Above them are smaller white streaks – icy clouds that race around the planet. One of these clouds, seen by the *Voyager 2* space probe, was named 'Scooter' because it scooted around the planet so fast.

38
Neptune is sometimes farther from the Sun than Pluto. Planets and dwarf planets go around the Sun on orbits (paths) that look like circles, but Pluto's path is more squashed. This sometimes brings it closer to the Sun than Neptune.

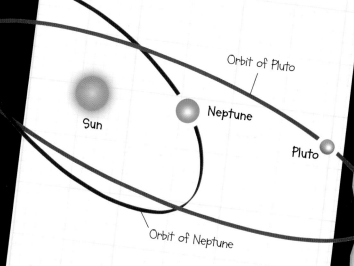

Orbit of Pluto

Sun

Neptune

Pluto

Orbit of Neptune

▲ Neptune is so far from the Sun that its orbit lasts 164.79 Earth years. It has only completed one orbit since it was discovered in 1846.

39 There are probably billions of tiny comets at the edge of the Solar System. They circle the Sun far beyond Neptune. Sometimes one is disturbed and moves inwards towards the Sun, looping around it before going back to where it came from. Some comets come back to the Sun regularly – Halley's comet returns every 76 years.

The solid part of a comet is hidden inside a huge, glowing cloud that stretches into a long tail.

40 A comet is often called a dirty snowball because it is made of dust and ice mixed together. Heat from the Sun melts some of the ice. This makes dust and gas stream away from the comet, forming a huge tail that glows in the sunlight.

41 Comet tails always point away from the Sun. Although it looks bright, a comet's tail is extremely thin s it is blown outwards, away from the Su When the comet moves away from the Sun, its tail goes in front of it.

42 Asteroids are chunks of rock that failed to stick together to make a planet. Most of them circle the Sun between Mars and Jupiter where there would be room for another planet. There are millions of asteroids, some the size of a car, and others as big as mountains.

ASTEROIDS

Asteroids travel in a ring around the Sun. This ring is called the asteroid belt and can be found between Mars and Jupiter.

43 Meteors are sometimes called shooting stars. They are not really stars, just streaks of light that flash across the night sky. Meteors are made when pebbles racing through space at high speed hit the top of the air above the Earth. The pebble gets so hot it burns up. We see it as a glowing streak for a few seconds.

▼ This crater in Arizona is one of the few large meteorite craters visible on Earth. The Moon is covered in them.

QUIZ
1. Which way does a comet tail always point?
2. What is another name for a meteor?
3. Where is the asteroid belt?

Answers:
1. Away from the Sun
2. Shooting star
3. Between Mars and Jupiter

A star is born

44 Stars are born in clouds of dust and gas called nebulae. Astronomers can see these clouds as shining patches in the night sky, or dark patches against the distant stars. These clouds shrink as gravity pulls the dust and gas together. At the centre, the gas gets hotter and hotter until a new star is born.

45 Stars begin their lives when they start making energy. When the dust and gas pulls tightly together it gets very hot. Finally it gets so hot in the middle that it can start making energy. The energy makes the star shine, giving out heat and light like the Sun.

KEY

1 Clumps of gas in a nebula start to shrink into the tight round balls that will become stars. The gas spirals round as it is pulled inwards.

2 Deep in its centre, the new star starts making energy, but it is still hidden by the cloud of dust and gas.

3 The dust and gas are blown away and we can see the star shining. Any left over gas and dust may form planets around the new star.

46 Young stars often stay together in clusters. When they start to shine they light up the nebula, making it glow with bright colours. Then the starlight blows away the remains of the cloud and we can see a group of new stars, called a star cluster.

STAR CLUSTER

This cluster of young stars, with many stars of different colours and sizes, will gradually drift apart, breaking up the cluster.

47 Large stars are very hot and white, smaller stars are cooler and redder. A large star can make energy faster and get much hotter than a smaller star. This gives them a very bright, bluish-white colour. Smaller stars are cooler. This makes them look red and shine less brightly. Ordinary in-between stars – like our Sun – look yellow.

②

48 Smaller stars live much longer than huge stars. Stars use up their gas to make energy, and the largest stars use up their gas much faster than smaller stars. The Sun is about halfway through its life. It has been shining for about 4.6 billion years and will go on shining for another 5 billion years.

③

Death of a star

49 Stars begin to die when they run out of gas to make energy. The middle of the star begins to shrink but the outer parts expand, making the star much larger.

At the end of their lives stars swell up into red giant stars, as shown in this far infrared image, or even larger red supergiants.

50 Red giant stars are dying stars that have swollen to hundreds of times their normal size. Their expanding outer layers get cooler, making them look red. When the Sun is a red giant it will be large enough to swallow up the nearest planets, Mercury and Venus, and perhaps Earth.

51 Eventually, a red giant's outer layers drift away, making a halo of gas around the star. The starlight makes this gas glow and we call it a planetary nebula. All that is left is a small, hot star called a white dwarf, which cannot make energy and gradually cools and dies.

PLANETARY NEBULA

This bow-tie shaped nebula is made by material cast off by a dying star as it enters its white dwarf phase.

WHITE DWARF STARS

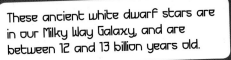

These ancient white dwarf stars are in our Milky Way Galaxy, and are between 12 and 13 billion years old.

52 Very heavy stars end their lives in a huge explosion called a supernova. This explosion blows away all the outer parts of the star. All that is left is a tiny hot star in the middle of a shell of hot glowing gas.

▶ Cassiopeia A is one of the best-studied supernova remnants. This image was made using data from three different types of telescopes.

I DON'T BELIEVE IT!

One of the main signs of a black hole is radiation from very hot gases near one just before they are sucked in.

53 After a supernova explosion the largest stars may end up as black holes. The remains of the star fall in on itself. As it shrinks, its gravity gets stronger. Eventually the pull of its gravity can get so strong that nothing near it can escape. This is called a black hole.

▲ Hot gas falling into a black hole called Cygnus X-1 gives out powerful X-rays picked up by the Chandra satellite.

Billions of galaxies

54 The Sun is part of a huge family of stars called the Milky Way Galaxy. There are billions of other stars in our galaxy, as many as the grains of sand on a beach. We call it the Milky Way because it looks like a very faint band of light in the night sky, as though someone has spilt some milk across space.

▶ With binoculars you can see that the faint glow of the Milky Way comes from millions of stars in our galaxy.

55 Curling arms give some galaxies their spiral shape. The Milky Way has arms made of bright stars and glowing clouds of gas that curl round into a spiral shape. Some galaxies, called elliptical galaxies, have a round shape like a squashed ball. Other galaxies have no particular shape.

I DON'T BELIEVE IT!
If you could fit the Milky Way onto these two pages, the Sun would be so tiny, you could not see it.

A CLUSTER OF GALAXIES

56 There are billions of galaxies outside the Milky Way. Some are larger than the Milky Way and many are smaller, but they all have more stars than you can count. The galaxies tend to stay together in groups called clusters.

Astronomers have nicknamed this interesting cluster of galaxies the 'Bullet Cluster'. It is made up of two colliding groups of galaxies.

ELLIPTICAL

SPIRAL

IRREGULAR

▲ Galaxies can be categorized by their shape. The Milky Way is a spiral galaxy.

57 There is no bump when galaxies collide. A galaxy is mostly empty space between the stars. But when galaxies get very close they can pull each other out of shape. Sometimes they look as if they have grown a huge tail stretching out into space, or their shape may change into a ring of glowing stars.

▲ These two galaxies are so close that each has pulled a long tail of bright stars from the other.

What is the Universe?

58 **The Universe is the name we give to everything we know about.** This means everything on Earth, from tiny bits of dust to the highest mountain, and everything that lives here. It also means everything in space – all the billions of stars in the billions of galaxies.

59 **The Universe started with a massive explosion called the Big Bang.** Astronomers think that this happened about 13.7 billion years ago. The explosion sent everything racing outwards in all directions. To start with, everything was packed incredibly close together. Over time it has expanded (spread out) into the Universe we can see today, which is mostly empty space.

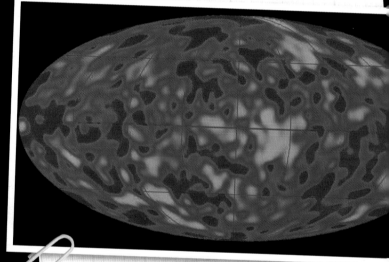

▲ A satellite has measured and mapped the oldest light in the Universe, known as the cosmic microwave background, providing a snapshot of the early Universe.

60 **The Universe's matter includes planets, stars and gas, and its energy includes light and heat.** Scientists suspect that it also contains unknown dark matter and dark energy, which we are unable to detect. These may affect what finally happens to the Universe.

DARK MATTER

Some of the distant galaxies in this cluster appear distorted, because light coming from them is being bent by invisible dark matter.

DOTTY UNIVERSE
You will need:
balloon   pen

Blow up a balloon a little, holding the neck to stop air escaping. Mark dots on the balloon with a pen, then blow it up some more. Watch how the dots move apart from each other. This is like the galaxies moving apart as the Universe expands.

61 The galaxies are still racing away from each other. When astronomers look at distant galaxies they can see that other galaxies are moving away from our galaxy, and the more distant galaxies are moving away faster. In fact all the galaxies are moving apart from each other. We say that the Universe is expanding.

62 We do not know what will happen to the Universe billions of years in the future. It may keep on expanding. If this happens, old stars will gradually die and no new ones will be born. Everywhere will become dark and cold.

KEY
1 All the parts that make up the Universe were once packed tightly together. No one knows why the Universe started expanding with a Big Bang.

2 As everything moved apart in all directions, stars and galaxies started to form.

3 Today there are galaxies of different shapes and sizes, all moving apart. One day they may start moving towards each other.

4 The Universe could stop expanding, or shrink and end with a Big Crunch.

Three, two, one... lift-off!

63 A rocket must travel nearly 40 times faster than a jumbo jet to blast into space. Slower than that, and gravity will pull it back to Earth. Rockets are powered by burning fuel, which makes hot gases. These gases rush out of the engines, shooting the rocket upwards.

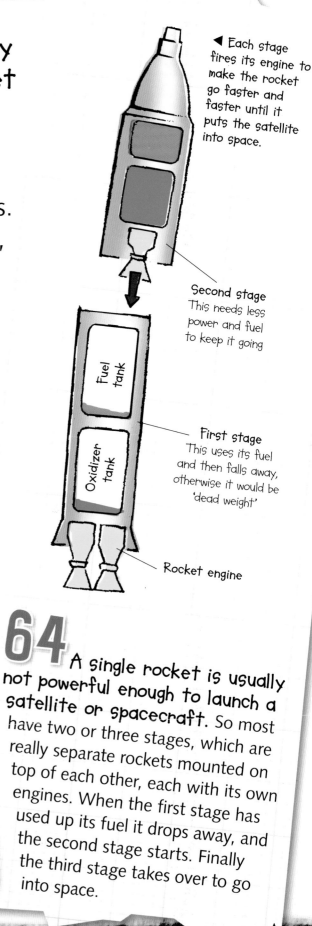

◄ Each stage fires its engine to make the rocket go faster and faster until it puts the satellite into space.

Second stage
This needs less power and fuel to keep it going

Fuel tank

First stage
This uses its fuel and then falls away, otherwise it would be 'dead weight'

Oxidizer tank

Rocket engine

The shuttle was blasted into space by three rocket engines and two huge booster rockets.

64 A single rocket is usually not powerful enough to launch a satellite or spacecraft. So most have two or three stages, which are really separate rockets mounted on top of each other, each with its own engines. When the first stage has used up its fuel it drops away, and the second stage starts. Finally the third stage takes over to go into space.

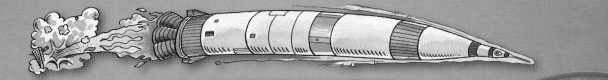

65

Some launchers have boosters. These are extra rockets fixed to the main one. Most boosters burn solid fuel, like giant firework rockets. They fall away when the fuel has burnt up. Some drift down on parachutes into the sea, to be used again.

QUIZ

1. Why did shuttles use parachutes — to stop or to start?
2. How many times faster than a jet does a rocket have to travel to blast into space?
3. What year was the final shuttle mission?

Answers:
1. To stop
2. Forty times faster 3. 2011

◄ On 8 July, 2011, space shuttle *Atlantis* took off from Florida, USA on the final mission of the 30-year space shuttle programme.

The shuttle puts down its wheels and lands on the runway. A parachute and speed brakes bring the shuttle to a standstill.

66

The space shuttles were re-usable spaceplanes. The first was launched in 1981 and there were more than 130 missions. The shuttle took off straight up like a rocket, carrying a load of up to 24 tonnes. To land it swooped down to glide onto a runway.

Living in space

67 Space is a dangerous place for astronauts. It can be boiling hot in the sunshine or freezing cold in the Earth's shadow. There is also dangerous radiation from the Sun. Dust, rocks and bits from other rockets race through space at such speed, they could easily make a small hole in a spacecraft, letting the air leak out.

▼ In a spacesuit, many layers of different materials are needed to keep the astronaut safe.

KEY
❶ Outer layers protect the wearer from the fierce heat of the Sun

❷ This layer seals the suit from the vacuum of space

❸ Soft lining goes next to the skin

❹ Tubes carrying cooling water

It is not easy for an astronaut wearing a bulky spacesuit to hold tools or bend his or her arms.

68 Spacesuits protect astronauts when they are out in space. They are very bulky because they are made of many layers to make them strong. They must hold the air for astronauts to breathe and protect them against speeding dust and harmful radiation. To keep the astronauts cool while they work outside the spacecraft, tubes of water under the spacesuit carry away heat.

SPACE MEALS

You will need:
dried noodles   boiling water

Buy a dried snack such as noodles, which just needs boiling water added. This is the kind of food astronauts eat. Most of their meals are dried so they are not too heavy to launch into space.

70 Everything floats around in space as if it has no weight. So all objects have to be fixed down or they will float away. Astronauts have footholds to keep them still while they are working. They strap themselves into sleeping bags so they don't bump into things when they are asleep.

69 Astronauts must take everything they need into space with them. Out in space there is no air, water or food, so all the things that astronauts need to live must be packed into their spacecraft and taken with them.

▶ Sleeping bags are fixed to walls so astronauts look as though they are asleep standing up.

71 A space station is a home in space for astronauts and cosmonauts (Russian astronauts). It has a kitchen for making meals, and cabins with sleeping bags. There are toilets, wash basins and sometimes showers. There are places to work, and controls where astronauts can check that everything is working properly.

▼ The Inter
Space Static
astronauts
home in spac
still being c
whilst in or

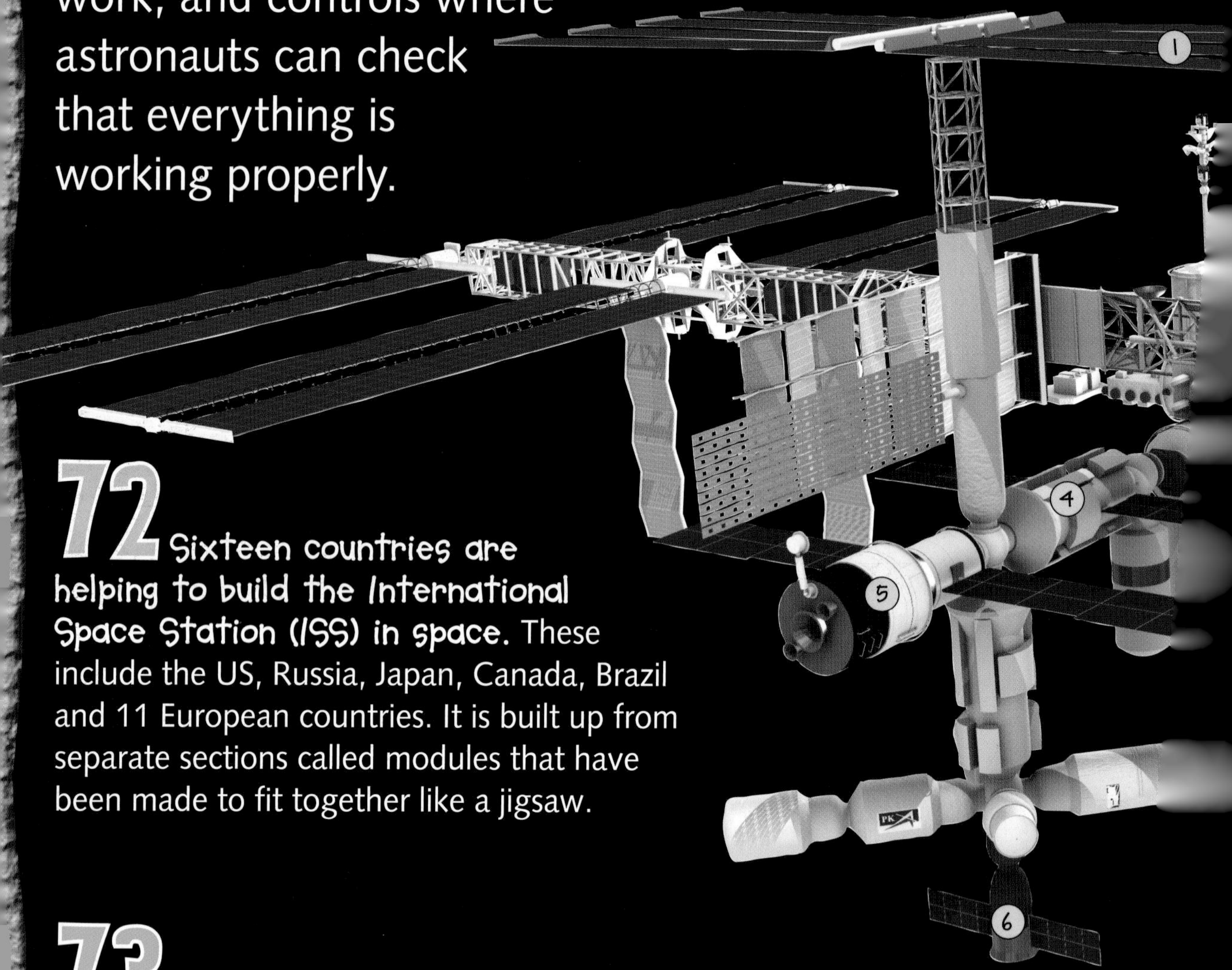

72 Sixteen countries are helping to build the International Space Station (ISS) in space. These include the US, Russia, Japan, Canada, Brazil and 11 European countries. It is built up from separate sections called modules that have been made to fit together like a jigsaw.

73 The US space station *Skylab*, launched in 1973, fell back to Earth in 1979. Most of it landed in the ocean but some pieces hit Australia.

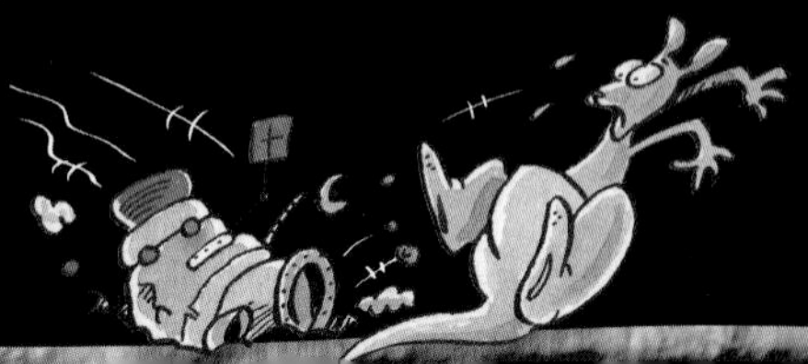

KEY

1. Solar panels for power
2. Space shuttle
3. Docking port
4. Control module
5. Living module
6. [illegible]

INTERNATIONAL SPACE STATION

74 Each part is launched from Earth and added to the ISS in space. There they are fitted by astronauts at the ISS with the help of a robot arm. Huge panels of solar cells have been added. These turn sunlight into electricity to provide a power supply for the space station.

An aerial view of a hurricane swirling on Earth is captured by an ISS crew member in September 2010.

75 The crew live on board the ISS for several months at a time. The first crew of three people arrived at the space station in November 2000 and stayed for over four months. When the space station is finished there will be room for seven astronauts and they will have six modules where they can live and work.

76 People and supplies can travel to the ISS in Russian Soyuz spacecraft. There are also robot ferries with no crew, including Russian Progress craft and European ATVs (Automated Transfer Vehicles). In 2001, American Dennis Tito became the first space tourist, staying on the ISS for eight days.

Robot explorers

77 Robot spacecraft called probes have explored all the planets. Probes take close-up pictures and measurements, and send the data back to scientists on Earth. Some probes circle planets taking pictures. For a really close-up look, a probe can land on the surface.

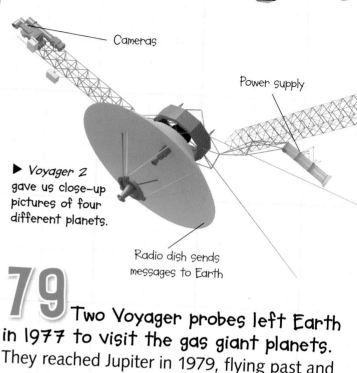

Cameras

Power supply

▶ *Voyager 2* gave us close-up pictures of four different planets.

Radio dish sends messages to Earth

78 In 1976, two Viking spacecraft landed on Mars to look for life. They scooped up some dust and tested it to see if any tiny creatures lived on Mars. They did not find any signs of life and their pictures showed only a dry, red, dusty desert.

79 Two Voyager probes left Earth in 1977 to visit the gas giant planets. They reached Jupiter in 1979, flying past and on to Saturn. *Voyager 2* then went on to visit Uranus in 1986 and Neptune in 1989. They sent back thousands of close-up pictures of each planet and its moons and rings as they flew past. They also discovered new rings and many new moons around the giant planets. Both Voyagers are now leaving the Solar System and will send back information about space between the stars until 2020.

◀ The Viking landers took soil samples from Mars, but found no signs of life.

80 The *Galileo* space probe arrived at Jupiter in 1995 and circled the planet for nearly 8 years. It found that two of its largest moons may have watery oceans hidden under their thick icy surfaces. *Juno* will be the next probe to visit Jupiter, aiming to find out more about how the giant planet formed.

▶ Called *Spirit* and *Opportunity*, the rovers are 2.3 metres wide and 1.5 metres tall to the cameras on their masts.

▲ The *Juno* space probe will arrive at Jupiter in 2016, and circle the planet to study its deep swirling clouds.

81 In 2003, two rockets launched the twin Mars Exploration Rovers (MERs) — remote-controlled robot vehicles. They landed on Mars in January 2004, and trundled around, taking pictures and gathering data. Another rover, named *Curiosity*, touched down in 2012 to search for evidence that Mars once supported life.

QUIZ

1. When did the Voyager probes fly past Jupiter?
2. How long did the *Galileo* probe circle Jupiter?
3. Which probes tested the dust on Mars for signs of life?
4. How tall are *Spirit* and *Opportunity*?

Answers:
1. 1979 2. 8 years
3. Viking 4. 1.5 metres

Watching the Earth

82 Hundreds of satellites circle the Earth in space. They are launched into space by rockets and may stay there for ten years or more.

▼ Weather satellites look down at the clouds and give warning when a violent storm is approaching.

83 Weather satellites help the forecasters tell us what the weather will be like. These satellites can see where the clouds are forming and which way they are going. They watch the winds and rain and measure how hot the air and the ground are.

▶ The different satellites each have their own job to do, looking at the Earth, or the weather, or out into space.

84 Communications satellites carry TV programmes and telephone messages around the world. Large aerials on Earth beam radio signals up to a space satellite that then beams them down to another aerial, half way round the world. This lets us talk to people on the other side of the world, and watch events such as the Olympics Games while they are happening in faraway countries.

▼ Communications satellites can beam TV programmes directly to your home through your own aerial dish.

85 Spy satellites circling the Earth take pictures of secret sites around the world. They can listen to secret radio messages from military ships or aircraft.

▶ Satellite telescopes let astronomers look far out into the Universe and discover what is out there.

▼ Pictures of the Earth taken by satellites can help make very accurate maps.

86 Earth-watching satellites look out for pollution. Oil slicks in the sea and dirty air over cities show up clearly in pictures from these satellites. They can help farmers by showing how well crops are growing and by looking for pests and diseases. Spotting forest fires and icebergs that may be a danger to ships is also easier from space.

87 Satellite telescopes let astronomers look at exciting things in space. They can see other kinds of radiation, such as X-rays, as well as light. X-ray telescopes can tell astronomers where there may be a black hole.

Voyage to the Moon

88 The first men landed on the Moon in 1969. They were two astronauts from the US Apollo 11 mission. Neil Armstrong was the first person to set foot on the Moon. Only five other Apollo missions have landed on the Moon since then.

89 The giant *Saturn 5* rocket launched the astronauts on their journey to the Moon. It was the largest rocket to have ever been built. Its three stages lifted the astronauts into space, and the third stage gave it an extra boost to send it to the Moon.

▲ In 1969, about half a billion people watched US astronaut Neil Armstrong's first steps onto another world.

Thrusters

Command Module

Lunar Module

Legs folded for journey

Main engine

Service Module with fuel and air supplies

▲ The Lunar and Command Modules travelled to the Moon fixed together, then separated for the Moon landing.

90 The Command Module that carried the astronauts to the Moon had no more room than an estate car. The astronauts were squashed inside it for the journey, which took three days to get there and another three to get back. On their return, the Command Module, with the astronauts inside, splashed down in the sea.

▼ Apollo 15, launched in 1971, was the fourth Apollo mission. Here, astronaut Jim Irwin loads the Lunar Rover (right). The Lunar Module is on the left.

91 The Lunar Module took two of the astronauts – Neil Armstrong and Edwin 'Buzz' Aldrin – to the Moon's surface. Once safely landed, they put on spacesuits and went outside to collect rocks. Later they took off in the Lunar Module to join the third astronaut – Michael Collins – who had stayed in the Command Module, circling above the Moon on his own.

92 The Lunar Rover was a moon car for the astronauts to ride on. It looked like a buggy with four wheels and two seats. It could only travel about as fast as you can run. The astronauts drove for up to 20 kilometres at a time, exploring the Moon's rocky surface near their landing site.

93 No one has been back to the Moon since the last Apollo mission left in 1972. Maybe one day people will return to the Moon and build bases where they can live and work.

94 On the way to the Moon in 1970, an explosion damaged the Apollo 13 spacecraft. This left the astronauts with little heat or light, but they managed to return safely to Earth.

Are we alone?

95 The only life we have found so far in the Universe is here on Earth. Everywhere you look on Earth from the frozen Antarctic to the hottest, driest deserts, on land and in the sea, there are living things. Some are huge, such as whales and elephants, and others are much too small to see. But they all need water to live.

▼ On Earth, animals can live in a wide range of different habitats, such as in the sea, in deserts and jungles, and icy lands.

DESERT

SEA

POLAR LANDS

RAINFOREST

Ocean

Rock shell

Icy surface

Metallic iron core

▲ Deep beneath Europa's cracked, icy surface, it may be warm enough for the ice to melt into water.

96 There may be an underground ocean on Europa, one of Jupiter's moons. Europa is a little smaller than our Moon and is covered in ice. However, astronomers think that there may be an ocean of water under the ice. If so, there could be strange living creatures swimming around deep underground.

▲ No one knows what other exoplanets would be like. They could have strange moons or colourful rings. Anything that lives there might look very strange to us.

97 Astronomers have found planets circling other stars, called exoplanets. Most of them are large, like Jupiter. But perhaps some could be smaller, like Earth. They could have a rocky surface that is not too hot or too cold, and suitable for liquid water – known as 'Goldilocks planets' after the fairytale character who tried the three bears' porridge. These planets could support some kind of life.

98 Mars seems to have had rivers and seas billions of years ago. Astronomers can see dry riverbeds and ridges that look like ocean shores on its surface. This makes them think Mars may have been warm and wet long ago and something may once have lived there. Now it is very cold and dry with no sign of life.

99 Our nearest neighbouring star is Proxima Centauri. This star is 4.2 light years away from Earth, which means it would take many thousands of years to reach it using today's spacecraft. Perhaps in the future scientists will discover how we can travel faster than the speed of light!

100 Each Pioneer probe carries a plaque about 23 centimetres wide. They show pictures of a man and woman, with the Solar System along the bottom and a chart of where the Earth is among the stars. In space the Pioneers will keep going forever, unless they hit something like a moon, a planet or an asteroid.

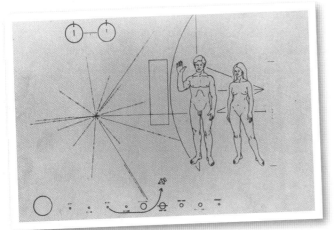

▲ Maybe the Pioneer plaques will be found by aliens who perhaps can read them and come to visit us!

ASTRONOMY

101 Astronomy is the study of everything you can see in the night sky and many other things out in space. Astronomers try to find out all about stars and galaxies. They look for planets circling around stars, and at mysterious explosions far out in space. Telescopes help them to see further, spotting things that are much too faint to see with just their eyes.

▼ New stars are forming in this cloud of dark dust and glowing gas in space. It is called the Pelican Nebula.

Families of stars

102 Stars are huge balls of hot gas. They look tiny to us because they are so far away. Deep in the centre of a star it is so hot that some of the gas turns into energy. Stars shine by sending out this energy as light and heat.

103 A star starts life in a cloud of dust and gas called a nebula. Thicker parts of the cloud collapse into a ball that becomes a star. Sometimes a star will shine until its gas is used up, and then swell into a red giant star. A large star may then explode as a supernova but smaller ones just shrink, becoming tiny white dwarf stars.

104 A star's colour shows how hot it is. Red stars are small and cool, yellow ones are bigger and hotter, and white ones are huge and very hot. Dying stars get even bigger, becoming giants or supergiants.

▶ The Milky Way Galaxy looks like a band of light, instead of a spiral shape, because we are looking through it from inside one of the spiral arms.

BUTTERFLY NEBULA

At the end of its life a red giant star threw out this glowing cloud of gas.

STAR CLUSTER

The Quintuplet cluster is a group of bright young stars. They shine with different colours – red, blue and white.

M81 GALAXY

This huge spiral galaxy contains billions of stars. Our Milky Way Galaxy would look like this if we could see it from above.

105 After it explodes as a supernova, a giant star may collapse, forming a black hole. The gravity of a black hole is so strong that it pulls everything into it – not even light can escape!

106 Galaxies are huge families of stars. Some are shaped like squashed balls, and these are called elliptical galaxies. Others have a spiral shape with arms curling out from a central ball of stars. Our Sun is in a spiral galaxy called the Milky Way. On very clear, dark nights you can see it as a faint band of light across the sky.

107 Using powerful telescopes, astronomers can see galaxies in all directions. They think there are many billions of galaxies, each containing billions of stars. All these stars and galaxies are part of the Universe. This is the name we give to everything we know about, including all the galaxies, our Sun and Moon, the Earth and everything on it, including you.

Starry skies

108 People have always been fascinated by the stars and Moon. Ancient people watched the Sun cross the sky during the day and disappear at night. Then when it got dark they saw the Moon and stars move across the sky. They wondered what caused these things to happen.

QUIZ

1. What was the Egyptian sun god called?
2. What did the Chinese see when they thought a dragon was eating the Sun?
3. What was a 'long haired star'?

Answers:
1. Ra 2. An eclipse 3. A comet

109 Sometimes the Sun goes dark in the middle of the day. This is called a solar eclipse, and it is caused by the Moon moving in front of the Sun, blocking its light. People in the past did not know this, so eclipses were scary. In ancient China, people thought they were caused by a dragon eating the Sun.

110 In ancient times people did not know what the Sun, Moon and stars were. Many thought the Sun was a god. The ancient Egyptians called this god Ra. They believed he rode across the sky in a boat each day and was swallowed by the sky goddess, Nut, every evening and then born again the next morning.

▲ The Egyptians pictured their sky goddess Nut with a starry body and their sun god Ra sitting on a throne.

◀ Ancient Chinese people fired arrows and banged pots and pans during eclipses, believing this would frighten the dragon away.

▲ The Bayeux Tapestry, made during the 1070s, shows people pointing at the famous Halley's comet (at the top right).

◀ The Greek sun god, Helios, rode across the sky in a chariot pulled by four horses.

111 Early astronomers could not predict when comets would appear. Comets were known as 'long-haired stars' because of their glowing tails, and many people thought they brought bad luck. They were blamed for disasters, from floods and famines to defeat in battle.

▶ Quetzalcoatl was a feathered serpent, and to the Aztec people of Central America he was the god of the morning star.

Mapping the stars

112 Ancient astronomers made maps of star patterns, dividing them into groups called constellations. People around the world all grouped the stars differently. Today, astronomers recognize 88 constellations that cover the whole sky.

▼ Old star maps showed the constellations as animals such as Draco the Dragon and Ursa Minor the Little Bear.

▼ The northern half of the Earth has different constellations from the southern half, but all the star patterns stay the same night after night.

NORTHERN HEMISPHERE

Ophiuchus (Serpent Bearer)
Aquila (Eagle)
Hercules (Strongman)
Serpens (Serpent)
Sagitta (Arrow)
Equuleus (Foal)
Lyra (Lyre)
Corona Borealis (Northern Crown)
Delphinus (Dolphin)
Boötes (Herdsman)
Draco (Dragon)
Cygnus (Swan)
Pegasus (Winged Horse)
Coma Berenices (Berenice's Hair)
Lacerta (Lizard)
Virgo (Virgin)
Canes Venatici (Hunting Dogs)
Cepheus (King)
Andromeda (Chained Princess)
Pisces (Fishes)
Leo (Lion)
Ursa Minor (Little Bear)
Ursa Major (Great Bear)
Cassiopeia (Queen)
Triangulum (Triangle)
Camelopardalis (Giraffe)
Leo Minor (Little Lion)
Aries (Ram)
Lynx (Lynx)
Perseus (Hero)
Cancer (Crab)
Hydra (Sea Serpent)
Auriga (Charioteer)
Cetus (Whale)
Gemini (Twins)
Taurus (Bull)
Canis Minor (Little Dog)
Orion (Hunter)

113 Astronomers gave names to the star patterns. Some are named after animals, including a bear, a lion, a swan, a dove, a crab and a snake. Others are named after gods and heroes. These include Orion (a hunter), Casseiopia (a queen), and the hero Perseus saving Princess Andromeda.

ASTRONOMY

◀ Here an ancient astronomer (bottom left) is pictured comically looking through the starry celestial sphere to see how it moves.

115 **Stars appear to move across the sky at night.** This is because the Earth is spinning all the time, but in the past people thought the stars were fixed to the inside of a huge hollow ball called the celestial sphere, which moved slowly around the Earth.

114 **Over 2000 years ago, the Greek astronomer Hipparchus made a catalogue of over 850 stars.** He listed their brightness and positions, and called the brightest ones first magnitude stars. Astronomers still call the brightness of a star its magnitude.

SPOT A STAR PATTERN

You will need:
clear night   warm clothes   dark place
good view of the sky

If you live in the North, look for the saucepan-shape of the Big Dipper – four stars for the bowl and three for the handle. If you live in the South, look overhead for four stars in the shape of a cross – the Southern Cross.

SOUTHERN HEMISPHERE

116 **Ancient astronomers noticed that one star seems to stay still while the others circle around it.** This is the Pole Star. It is above the North Pole and shows which direction is north. The ancient Egyptians used this knowledge to align the sides of the pyramids exactly.

53

Keeping time

Day 1

Day 3
Crescent
Moon

Day 5

Day 7
Half Moon

Day 10

Day 14
Full Moon

Day 17

Day 19

Day 21
Half Moon

Day 24

Day 26
Crescent
Moon

Day 28
New Moon

▲ The Moon's changing shapes are called the phases of the Moon. It doesn't really change shape – it is always a round ball of rock.

117 The Sun, Moon and stars can be used to measure time. It takes a day for the Earth to spin round, and a year for it to circle the Sun. By observing changes in the positions of constellations, astronomers worked out the length of a year so they could make a calendar.

118 It takes 29.5 days for the Moon to circle the Earth. The Moon seems to change shape because we see different amounts of its sunlit side as it goes round the Earth. When the sunlit side faces Earth we see a Full Moon. When it faces away, we see only a thin crescent shape.

119

Ancient people used sundials to tell the time. A sundial consists of an upright rod and a flat plate. When the Sun shines, the rod casts a shadow on the plate. As the Sun moves across the sky, the shadow moves round the plate. Marks on the plate indicate the hours.

120

As the Earth circles the Sun, different stars appear in the sky. This helped people predict when seasons would change. In ancient Egypt the bright star Sirius showed when the river Nile would flood, making the land ready for crops.

MAKE A SUNDIAL

You will need:
short stick   plasticine   card
pencil   clock

1. Stand the stick upright on the card using the plasticine. Put it outside on a sunny day.
2. Every hour, make a pencil mark on the card where the shadow ends.
3. Leave the card where it is and the shadow will point to the time whenever the Sun is out.

▼ The shadow made by this sundial points to the time, which is marked on the round dial.

◄ Stonehenge's huge upright stones are lined up with sunrise on the longest day in midsummer and on the shortest day in midwinter.

121

Stonehenge is an ancient monument in England that is lined up with the Sun and Moon. It is a circle of giant stones over 4000 years old. It may have been used as a calendar, or an observatory to predict when eclipses would happen.

Wandering stars

122 When people began to study the stars they spotted five that were unlike the rest. Instead of staying in fixed patterns, they moved across the constellations, and they did not twinkle. Astronomers called them planets, which means 'wandering stars'.

123 The planets are named after ancient Roman gods. Mercury is the messenger of the gods, Venus is the god of love, Mars is the god of war, Jupiter is king of the gods and Saturn is the god of farming. Later astronomers used telescopes to find two more planets, and named them Uranus and Neptune after the gods of the sky and the sea.

124 At first people thought that the Earth was at the centre of everything. They believed the Sun, Moon and planets all circled the Earth. The ancient Greek astronomer Ptolemy thought the Moon was nearest Earth, then Mercury and Venus, then the Sun, and finally Jupiter and Saturn.

▼ Ptolemy's picture of the Solar System shows the Earth in the middle and the Sun and planets moving round it in circles.

DRAW AN ELLIPSE

You will need:
two drawing pins   paper   thick card   pencil   string

1. Place the paper on the card. Push the pins into the paper, placing them a little way apart.
2. Tie the string into a loop that fits loosely round the pins.
3. Using the pencil point, pull the string tight into a triangle shape.
4. Move the pencil round on the paper, keeping the string tight to draw an ellipse.

125

Astronomers measured the positions and movements of the planets. What they found did not fit Ptolemy's ideas. In 1543, the Polish astronomer Nicolaus Copernicus suggested that the planets circled the Sun. This explained much of what the astronomers saw, but still didn't fit the measurements exactly.

◀ Nicolaus Copernicus' view placed the Sun in the middle with the Earth moving round it with the other planets.

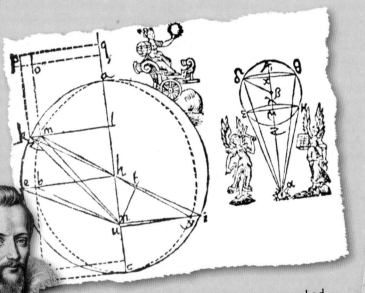

▲ Kepler's drawing shows how he worked out that the planets move along ellipses, not circles.

126

German astronomer Johannes Kepler published his solution to this problem in 1609. He realized that the orbits of Earth and the planets were not perfect circles, but ellipses (slightly squashed circles). This fitted all the measurements and describes the Solar System as we know it today.

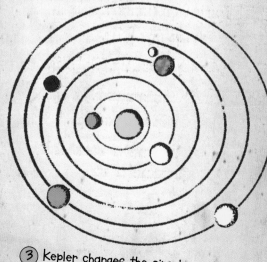

① From above, Ptolemy's plan shows everything (from inside to outside: Earth's Moon, Mercury, Venus, Sun, Mars, Jupiter, Saturn) moving round the Earth.

② Copernicus' view changes this to show everything moving round the Sun.

③ Kepler changes the circular paths of the planets into ellipses.

First telescopes

127 The telescope was invented in about 1608. Telescopes use two lenses (discs of glass that bulge out in the middle, or curve inwards) – one at each end of a tube. When you look through a telescope, distant things look nearer and larger.

128 Italian scientist Galileo built a telescope in 1609. He was one of the first people to use the new invention for astronomy. With it, Galileo observed craters and mountains on the Moon, and discovered four moons circling the planet Jupiter. He was also amazed to see many more stars in the sky.

▲ Galileo shows a crowd of people the exciting new things he can see through his telescope.

Mirror

JUPITER

IO

EUROPA

129 When Galileo looked at the planet Venus through his telescope he saw that it sometimes appeared to be crescent shaped, just like the Moon. This meant that Venus was circling the Sun and not the Earth and helped to prove that Copernicus was right about the planets circling the Sun. Galileo described his amazing discoveries in a book called *The Starry Messenger.*

▲ Jupiter's four largest moons are called the Galilean moons, because Galileo was the first person to see them using his telescope.

CALLISTO

GANYMEDE

130 Other astronomers were soon trying to build more powerful telescopes. In 1668, English scientist Isaac Newton made one in which he replaced one of the lenses with a curved mirror, shaped like a saucer. He had invented the reflecting telescope. Large modern telescopes are based on Newton's invention.

131 According to legend, Newton began to think about gravity when he saw an apple fall from a tree. He wondered why the apple fell down to the ground instead of floating upwards.

132 Newton also worked out why the planets orbit the Sun. He realized that something was pulling the planets towards the Sun – a pulling force called gravity. The pull of the Sun's gravity keeps the planets in their orbits, and the Earth's gravity holds the Moon in its orbit. It also prevents everything on Earth from floating off into space.

Eyepiece

Sliding focus

Ball mounting

◀ The mirror in Newton's telescope gave a clearer image of the stars than telescopes with lenses.

Discoveries with telescopes

▶ Halley's comet was last seen in 1986 and will return again in 2061.

133 Astronomers made many new discoveries with their telescopes. The English astronomer Edmund Halley was interested in comets. He thought that a bright comet seen in 1682 was the same as one that was seen in 1607, and predicted that it would return in 1758. His prediction was right and the comet was named after him – Halley's Comet.

◀ Halley also mapped the stars and studied the Sun and Moon.

▼ The Orion Nebula, a huge glowing cloud of gas, is Messier's object number 42.

134 The French astronomer Charles Messier was also a comet hunter. In 1781 he tried to make his search easier by listing over 100 fuzzy objects in the sky that could be mistaken for comets. Later astronomers realized that some of these are glowing clouds of dust and gas and others are distant galaxies.

▲ Messier's object number 16 is the Eagle Nebula, a dusty cloud where stars are born.

▼ Messier's object number 31 is a giant spiral galaxy called Andromeda.

135 William Herschel, a German astronomer living in England, discovered a new planet in 1781. Using a reflecting telescope he had built himself, he spotted a star that seemed to move. It didn't look like a comet, and Herschel realized that it must be a new planet. It was the first planet discovered with a telescope and was called Uranus.

▲ William Herschel worked as astronomer for King George III of England.

136 Astronomers soon discovered that Uranus was not following its expected orbit. They thought another planet might be pulling it off course. Following predictions made by mathematicians, astronomers found another planet in 1846. It was called Neptune. It is so far away that it looks like a star.

137 The discovery of Neptune didn't fully explain Uranus' orbit. In 1930 an American astronomer, Clyde Tombaugh, found Pluto. It was the ninth planet from the Sun and much smaller than expected. In 2006 astronomers decided to call Pluto a dwarf planet.

▲ Herschel's great telescope was the largest telescope in the world at the time and its mirror measured 1.2 metres across.

QUIZ

1. Who discovered the planet Uranus?
2. When was Halley's Comet last seen?
3. Which was the ninth planet from the Sun until 2006?

Answers:
1. William Herschel 2. 1986
3. Pluto

How telescopes work

138 **Telescopes make distant things look nearer.** Most stars are so far away that even with a telescope they just look like points of light. But the Moon and planets seem much larger through a telescope – you can see details such as craters on the Moon and cloud patterns on Jupiter.

139 **A reflecting telescope uses a curved mirror to collect light.** The mirror reflects and focuses the light. A second, smaller mirror sends the light out through the side of the telescope or back through a hole in the big mirror to an eyepiece lens. Looking through the eyepiece lens you see a larger image of the distant object.

Eyepiece lens

Reflected light

▶ Star light bounces off the main mirror of a reflecting telescope back up to the eyepiece lens near the top.

Secondary mirror

Light enters

Primary mirror

140 **A telescope that uses a lens instead of a mirror to collect light is called a refracting telescope.** The lens focuses the light and it goes straight down the telescope tube to the eyepiece lens at the other end. Refracting telescopes are not as large as reflecting ones because large lenses are very heavy.

Focused light

Eyepiece lens

141
Astronomers are building telescopes with larger and larger mirrors. Bigger mirrors reveal fainter objects so telescopes can see further and further into the Universe. They also show more details in the distant galaxies and the wispy glowing clouds between the stars.

142
Today, professional astronomers don't look through their telescopes. They use cameras to capture the images. A camera can build up an image over a long time. The light adds up to make a brighter image, showing things that could not be seen by just looking through the telescope.

▲ A telescope reveals round craters on the Moon and large dark patches called 'seas' although the Moon is completely dry.

▲ The mirror from the Rosse Telescope in Ireland is 1.8 metres across and is kept in the Science Museum in London. One hundred years ago it was the largest telescope in the world.

▼ In a refracting telescope the main lens at the top bends the light, making an image near the bottom of the telescope.

Primary lens

Light enters

I DON'T BELIEVE IT!
The Liverpool telescope on the island of La Palma in the Atlantic Ocean is able to automatically observe a list of objects sent to it via the Internet.

Telescopes today

143 All large modern telescopes are reflecting telescopes. To make clear images, their mirrors must be exactly the right shape. The mirrors are made of polished glass, covered with a thin layer of aluminium to reflect as much light as possible. Some are made of thin glass that would sag without supports beneath to hold it in exactly the right shape.

144 Large telescope mirrors are often made up of many smaller mirrors. The mirrors of the Keck telescopes in Hawaii are made of 36 separate parts. Each has six sides, which fit together to make a mirror 10 metres across – about the width of a tennis court. The small mirrors are tilted to make exactly the right shape.

145 The air above a telescope is constantly moving. This can make their images blurred. Astronomers reduce this by using an extra mirror that can change shape. A computer works out what shape this mirror needs to be to remove the blurring effect and keeps changing it every few seconds. This is called adaptive optics.

▶ A huge frame holds the mirrors of a large reflecting telescope in position while tilting and turning to point at the stars.

Light enters

Secondary mirror

Reflected light

Primary mirror

Frame

▲ The main mirror of the Gran Telescopio Canarias telescope measures 10.4 metres across when all its 36 separate parts are fitted together.

146
Large telescopes can work together to see finer detail than a single telescope. When the two Keck telescopes are linked, they produce images that are almost as good as a telescope with a mirror as wide as the distance between them – 85 metres, (about the length of a football field).

147
Telescopes must be able to move to track the stars. It may take hours to make an image of a very faint, distant target and during this time the target will move gradually across the sky. Motors drive the telescope at just the right speed to keep it pointing at the target. All the time the image is being recorded using CCDs like those in an ordinary digital camera.

QUIZ
1. What are telescope mirrors made of?
2. How many sides does each piece of a Keck telescope mirror have?
3. Why do telescopes have to move?

Answers:
1. Glass 2. 6
3. To track the stars

▶ This picture of Saturn was taken by one of the Keck telescopes. The orange colours have been added to show the different temperatures in its clouds and rings.

Observatories

148 Observatories are places for watching the skies, often where telescopes are built and housed. There are usually several telescopes of different sizes at one observatory. Astronomers choose remote places far from cities, as bright lights can spoil observations.

149 Observatories are often on the tops of mountains and in dry desert areas. This is because the air close to the ground is constantly moving and full of clouds and dust. Astronomers need very clear, dry, still air so they build their telescopes as high as possible above most of the clouds and dust.

▶ The Gemini North telescope is one of the telescopes at the Mauna Kea Observatories in Hawaii. It has a twin called Gemini South in Chile, South America.

150 A desert is a good place to build an observatory.

The high mountains in the Atacama Desert, in Chile, South America, are among the driest places on Earth, and night skies there are incredibly dark. Several large telescopes have been built there including the Very Large Telescope (VLT).

▲ The Very Large Telescope is really four large telescopes and four smaller ones. The large telescopes are inside the square domes.

151 Some famous observatories are on top of a dormant volcano called Mauna Kea, on the island of Hawaii.

It is the highest mountain on an island in the world – most clouds are below it. It is a good place for astronomy because the air is very clean and dry. It has more clear nights than most other places on Earth. It has 13 telescopes, four of them very large.

Telescope inside

Raised shutter

Rotating dome

Building linking telescopes

▲ The two Keck telescopes at the Mauna Kea Observatories each have their own round dome with shutters that open to let in the starlight.

The Keck telescopes

▼ Observatories on Mauna Kea, Hawaii.

152 Domes cover the telescopes to protect them and keep the mirrors clean.

The domes have shutters that open when the telescopes are operating to let in the starlight. They also turn round so that the telescope can point in any direction and can move to track the stars.

Splitting light

153 Astronomers find out about distant stars by studying the starlight that reaches Earth. They can get more data from the light by splitting it into its different colours – like a rainbow that forms when raindrops split up sunlight. These colours are called a spectrum.

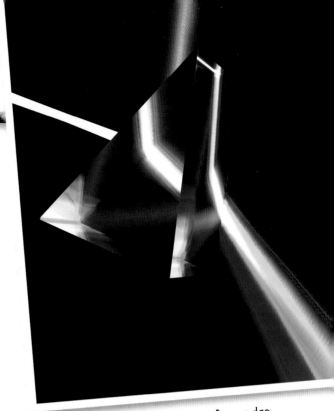

▲ White light going in one side of a wedge-shaped glass prism spreads out into a rainbow of colours, making a spectrum.

RAINBOW SPECTRUM

You will need:
drinking glass   small mirror
water   torch   card

1. Put the mirror in the glass so that it faces upwards.
2. Pour water into the glass to cover the mirror.
3. In a dark room, shine the torch onto the mirror.
4. Hold the card to catch the reflected light from the mirror and see a rainbow – the water and mirror have split the light into a spectrum.

154 Astronomers can tell how hot a star is from its spectrum. The hottest are blue-white, the coolest are red, and in between are yellow and orange stars. The spectrum also shows how big and bright the star is so astronomers can tell which are ordinary stars and which are red giants or supergiants.

155 A star's spectrum can show what gases the star is made of. Each gas has a different pattern of lines in the spectrum. Astronomers can also use the spectrum to find out which different gases make up a cloud of gas, by looking at starlight that has travelled through the cloud.

▶ Astronomers divide stars into classes from O, largest and hottest, to M, smallest and coolest.

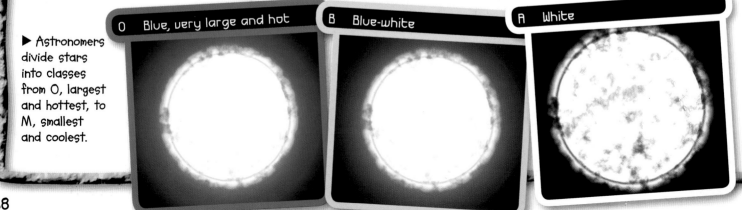

O   Blue, very large and hot   B   Blue-white   A   White

156 If a star or galaxy is moving away from Earth, its light is stretched out. This shows up in its spectrum and astronomers call it red shift. They use it to work out how fast a galaxy is moving and how far away it is. If the galaxy is moving towards Earth, the light gets squashed together and shows up in its spectrum as blue shift.

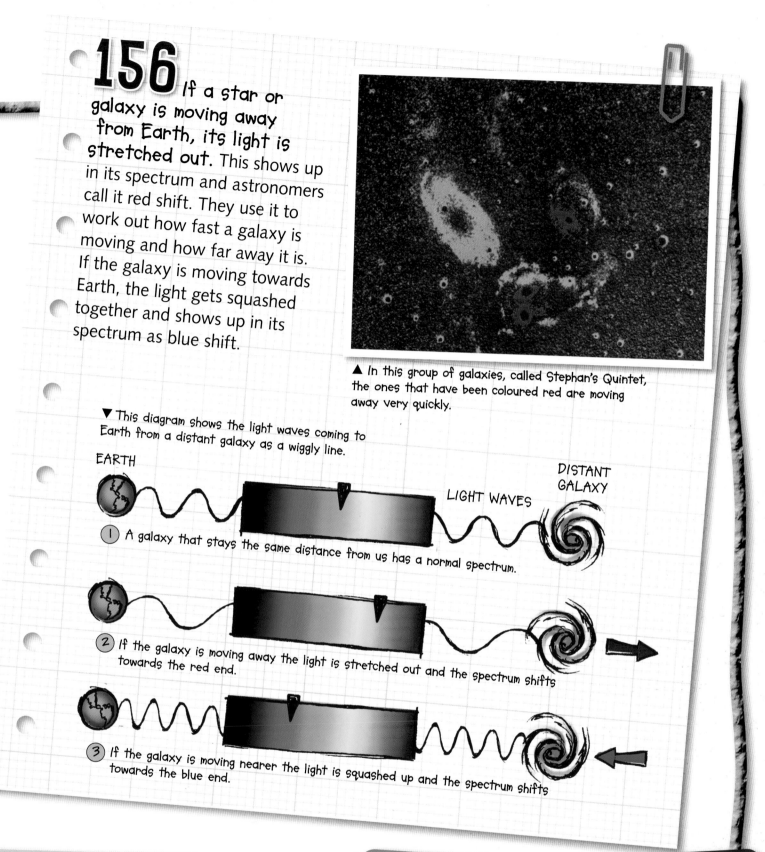

▲ In this group of galaxies, called Stephan's Quintet, the ones that have been coloured red are moving away very quickly.

▼ This diagram shows the light waves coming to Earth from a distant galaxy as a wiggly line.

EARTH

LIGHT WAVES

DISTANT GALAXY

① A galaxy that stays the same distance from us has a normal spectrum.

② If the galaxy is moving away the light is stretched out and the spectrum shifts towards the red end.

③ If the galaxy is moving nearer the light is squashed up and the spectrum shifts towards the blue end.

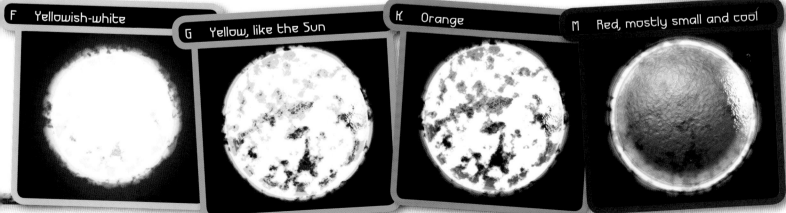

| F | Yellowish-white | G | Yellow, like the Sun | K | Orange | M | Red, mostly small and cool |

69

Space telescopes

157 Galaxies and stars send out other kinds of radiation, as well as light. Some send out radio waves like the ones that carry TV signals. There are also X-rays, like the kind that hospitals use to show broken bones, infrared light, gamma rays and ultra-violet light. They all carry information.

159 The Hubble space telescope is like a normal telescope, but it is above the air. Its images are much clearer than if it were on the ground. It has produced images of distant gas clouds showing star birth, and looked deep into space at galaxies that have never been seen before.

▶ The Hubble space telescope was launched into orbit around the Earth in 1990 and is still sending astronomers amazing images from space.

158 Some kinds of radiation are detected more easily by telescopes in space. This is because the air around Earth stops most radiation from reaching the ground, which is good, because it would be harmful to life on Earth. Space telescopes orbit Earth to collect the radiation and send the information down to Earth.

QUIZ
1. What kind of radiation can spot newborn stars?
2. Which space telescopes collect gamma rays from space?
3. What kind of radiation can spot black holes?

Answers:
1. Infrared radiation
2. The Fermi and Integral Gamma-ray Telescopes 3. X-rays and gamma rays

This picture includes data from Hubble (coloured green and dark blue), Spitzer (coloured red) and Chandra (coloured pale blue).

160
The space telescopes Chandra X-ray Observatory and XMM Newton both collect X-rays. The X-rays come from very hot gas inside huge galaxy clusters. They also reveal black holes, because gas swirling around black holes gets so hot that it gives out X-rays.

◄ For over ten years the Chandra X-ray Observatory has orbited the Earth looking at black holes and exploding stars.

161
Infrared light is picked up by the Spitzer and Herschel space telescopes. It comes from cool stars and clouds of dust and gas. Infrared light can be used to see through dust clouds around newborn stars, and around young stars where new planets may be forming. It also reveals the centre of our galaxy, which is hidden by dust.

► The Spitzer space telescope must be kept very cold so it can pick out the infrared light from distant galaxies.

162
The Fermi Gamma-ray Space Telescope and Integral are telescopes that collect gamma rays. These rays come from violent events in space such as huge explosions when stars blow up or collide. Like X-rays, gamma rays can also reveal black holes.

Radio telescopes

163 Radio waves from space are collected by radio telescopes. Most radio waves can travel through the air, so these telescopes are built on the ground. But there are lots of radio waves travelling around the Earth, carrying TV and radio signals, and phone calls. These can all interfere with the faint radio waves from space.

164 Radio telescopes work like reflecting telescopes, but instead of using a mirror, waves are collected by a big metal dish. They look like huge satellite TV aerials. Most dishes can turn to point at targets anywhere in the sky, and can track targets moving across the sky.

▶ Each radio telescope dish in the Very Large Array measures 25 metres across and can tilt and turn to face in different directions.

165

Some scientists use radio telescopes to listen out for messages from aliens on other planets or in other galaxies. They have not found any yet.

166

We can't see radio waves, but astronomers turn the signals into images we can see. The images from a single radio telescope dish are not very detailed but several radio telescopes linked together can reveal finer details. The Very Large Array (VLA) in New Mexico, USA, has 27 separate dishes arranged in a 'Y' shape, all working together as though it was one huge dish 36 kilometres across.

▶ These two orange blobs are clouds of hot gas on either side of a galaxy. They are invisible to ordinary telescopes but radio telescopes can reveal them.

167

Radio waves come from cool gas between the stars. This gas is not hot enough to glow so it can't be seen by ordinary telescopes. Radio telescopes have mapped clouds of gas showing the shape of the Milky Way Galaxy. They have also discovered what seems to be a massive black hole at its centre.

168

Radio waves reveal massive jets of gas shooting out from distant galaxies. The jets are thrown out by giant black holes in the middle of some galaxies, which are gobbling up stars and gas around them.

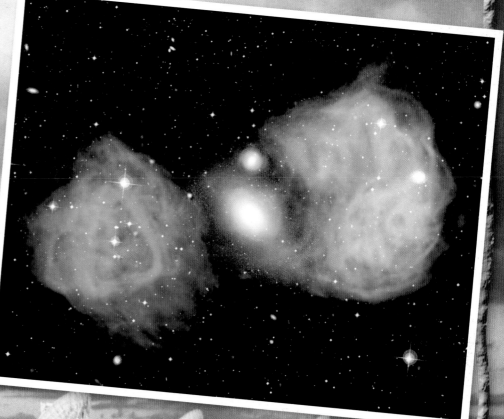

Watching the Sun

169 The Sun is our closest star and astronomers study it to learn about other stars. Without the Sun's light and heat nothing could live on the Earth, so astronomers keep a close eye on it. Tongues of very hot gas called flares and prominences often shoot out from the Sun.

▼ A loop of glowing gas called a prominence ❶ arches away from the Sun. Sun spots ❷ look dark because they are cooler that the rest of the surface.

170 Particles constantly stream out from the surface of the Sun in all directions. This is called the solar wind. Sometimes a huge burst of particles, called a Coronal Mass Ejection (CME), breaks out. If one comes towards Earth it could damage satellites and even telephone and power lines. CMEs can be dangerous for astronauts in space.

171 There are often dark patches on the Sun. These are cooler areas, and are called sunspots. The number of sunspots changes over time. Every 11 years numbers increase to a maximum of 100 or more, then in between the numbers go down to very few, or even none.

① Wispy gas surrounds the Sun (coloured blue) in this image from the SOHO spacecraft. **②** SOHO captures a Coronal Mass Ejection exploding out from the Sun.

172 A spacecraft called SOHO has been watching the Sun since 1995. It orbits the Sun between the Earth and the Sun, sending data and images back to Earth. It warns of changes in solar wind and of CMEs that could hit Earth, and has spotted many comets crashing into the Sun.

173 The Sun is losing weight! Every second, about 4 million tonnes of its gas is turned into energy and escapes as light and heat. The Sun is so big that it can continue losing weight at this rate for about another 5 billion years.

174 STEREO are a pair of spacecraft that look at the Sun. They orbit the Sun, one each side of the Earth, to get a 3D view. Like SOHO, they are looking for storms on the Sun that could affect the Earth. Information from STEREO is helping astronomers to work out why these storms happen.

▶ This illustration shows the two Stereo spacecraft soon after they were launched in 2006. They moved apart until they were on either side of the Earth.

The edge of the Universe

175 Astronomers think that the Universe started in a huge explosion they call the Big Bang. They know that distant galaxies are all moving further apart so the Universe must have been squashed tightly together billions of years ago. They think that some kind of explosion sent everything flying apart about 13.7 billion years ago.

176 As astronomers look further away they are also looking back in time. This is because light takes time to travel across the vast distances in space. It takes over four years for light to reach Earth from the second-nearest star (after the Sun), so we see this star as it was when the light left it four years ago. Light can take billions of years to travel from distant galaxies, so astronomers are looking back at the Universe as it was billions of years ago.

4 Our Sun and the Solar System formed after about 9 billion years

3 Stars and galaxies appeared after about 200–600 million years

9 billion yrs

2 After 300,000 years atoms started to form

300 million yrs

300,000 yrs

1 The Universe was unimaginably hot and tiny at first but cooled as it expanded

▶ This shows the Universe as it expanded and changed from the Big Bang to the present day.

◀ A map of the Cosmic Background Radiation shows tiny differences in temperature, the red areas are slightly warmer and the blue areas cooler.

177 Astronomers have found faint radiation coming from all over the sky. They call this the Cosmic Background Radiation. It is the remains of radiation left by the Big Bang explosion and helps to prove that the Big Bang really happened. Astronomers send satellites up to map this radiation and find out more about the Universe when it was very young.

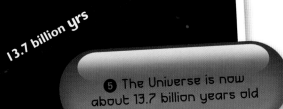

13.7 billion yrs

5 The Universe is now about 13.7 billion years old

▲ These galaxies are so far away that we are seeing them as they were billions of years ago when the Universe was much younger.

178 Astronomers use their biggest telescopes and space telescopes to try and find the most distant galaxies. They do not know how soon after the Big Bang the first stars and galaxies appeared and whether they were different from the stars and galaxies they see today. The Hubble space telescope has taken images of very faint faraway galaxies showing astronomers what the early Universe was like.

Up close

179 The planets and our Moon have all been explored by space probes. These travel through space carrying cameras and other instruments with which they can gather data. They then send all the information and images back to astronomers on Earth.

180 Some space probes fly past planets, gathering information. The *Voyager 2* space probe flew past the four giant planets (Jupiter, Saturn, Uranus and Neptune) in turn between 1979 and 1989. Astronomers now know much more about these planets from the detailed information and images *Voyager 2* sent back.

VOYAGER 2

▶ *Voyager 2* sent back this picture of Callisto, one of Jupiter's large moons.

Launch date: 20 August, 1977
Mission: Flew past Jupiter in 1979, Saturn in 1981, Uranus in 1986 and Neptune in 1989. Now flying out of the Solar System into deep space.

181 Space probes can orbit a planet to study it for longer. The probe *Cassini* went into orbit round Saturn. It carried a smaller probe that dropped onto Saturn's largest moon, Titan, to look at its surface, which is hidden by cloud. The main probe circled Saturn, investigating its moons and rings.

182 Venus is hidden by clouds, but the *Magellan* probe was able to map its surface. The probe sent radio signals through the clouds to bounce off the surface. It then collected the return signal. This is called radar. It revealed that Venus has many volcanoes.

CASSINI

▶ Saturn and its rings, taken by the *Cassini* spacecraft as it approached the planet.

Launch date: 15 October, 1997
Mission: Arrived at Saturn in 2004. Dropped Huygens probe onto Saturn's largest moon, Titan, then went into orbit to explore Saturn, its rings and moons.

SPIRIT AND OPPORTUNITY

183 Some probes land on a planet's surface. The probes *Spirit* and *Opportunity* explored the surface of Mars. They move slowly, stopping to take pictures and analyze rocks. They have discovered that although Mars is very dry now, there may have once been water on the surface.

Launch date: 10 June, 2003 (Spirit) and 7 July, 2003 (Opportunity)
Mission: After landing on Mars in January 2004 the two rovers drove across the surface testing the rocks and soil and sending back images and data.

▲ Among the many rocks scattered across the dusty Martian landscape *Spirit* found a rock that could have crashed down from space.

Astronomy from home

184 Many people enjoy astronomy as a hobby. You need warm clothes and somewhere dark, away from street and house lights, and a clear night. After about half an hour your eyes adjust to the dark so you can see more stars. A map of the constellations will help you find your way around the night sky.

185 Binoculars reveal even more stars and show details on the Moon. It is best to look at the Moon when it is half full. Craters, where rocks have crashed into the Moon, show up along the dark edge down the middle of the Moon. Binoculars also show Jupiter's moons as spots of light on or either side of the planet.

186 Telescopes are usually more powerful than binoculars and show fainter stars. They also show more detail in faint gas clouds called nebulae. Amateurs use reflecting and refracting telescopes, mounted on stands to keep them steady.

187 A camera can be fixed to a telescope to photograph the sky. A camera can build up an image over time if the telescope moves to follow the stars. The images show details that you could not see by just looking through the telescope.

KIT LIST
* Star map
* Red light torch
* Deckchair
* Warm clothes
* Pencil and notebook
* Blanket or sleeping bag
* Binoculars
* Telescope

SPOT VENUS
Venus is the brightest planet and easy to spot – it is known as the 'evening star'. Look towards the west in the twilight just after the Sun has set. The first bright 'star' to appear will often be Venus.

▼ In November each year amateur astronomers look out for extra shooting stars during the Leonid meteor shower.

▲ In 1997 the bright Comet Hale Bopp could be seen easily without a telescope or binoculars.

188
Meteors, also called shooting stars, look like streaks of light in the sky. They are made when tiny pieces of space rock and dust hit the air around the Earth and burn up. Several times during the year there are meteor showers when many shooting stars are seen. You can spot meteors without a telescope or binoculars.

▶ An amateur astronomer uses binoculars to see the many stars in the Milky Way.

189
Amateurs can collect useful information for professional astronomers. They are often the first to spot a new comet in the sky. Comets are named after the person who found them and some amateur astronomers even specialize in comet-spotting. Others watch variable stars and keep records of the changes in their brightness.

In the future

190 Kepler is a new satellite built specially to look for stars that might have planets where there could be life. So far, astronomers have not found life anywhere else in the Solar System. Kepler was launched in 2009 and is looking at stars to see if any of them have any planets like Earth.

▶ A Delta II rocket launches the Kepler spacecraft in March 2009 on its mission to hunt for distant planets.

I DON'T BELIEVE IT!

Astronomers are planning a new radio telescope, to be built in either Australia or South Africa. It is called the Square Kilometre Array and will have at least 3000 separate radio telescopes. It should start working in 2020.

191 ALMA (short for Atacama Large Millimetre Array) is a powerful new radio telescope being built high up in the Atacama Desert in Chile. When it is complete in 2012 it will have 66 radio dishes linked together to make one huge radio telescope.

192

The James Webb Space Telescope will replace the Hubble Space telescope in 2014. Its mirror will be 6.5 metres across, nearly three times wider than Hubble's main mirror. This will not fit in a rocket so it will be made of 18 separate mirrors that will unfold and fit together once the telescope is in space.

▲ A large sunshield will keep the mirrors of the James Webb telescope cool so it can make images using infrared light.

193

Several new giant telescopes are being planned. The Thirty Meter Telescope will have a mirror 30 metres across – about the length of three double-decker buses. This will be made of 492 smaller mirrors. The European Extremely Large Telescope will have an even larger mirror, 42 metres across, made of 984 separate mirrors. Both should be ready to use in 2018.

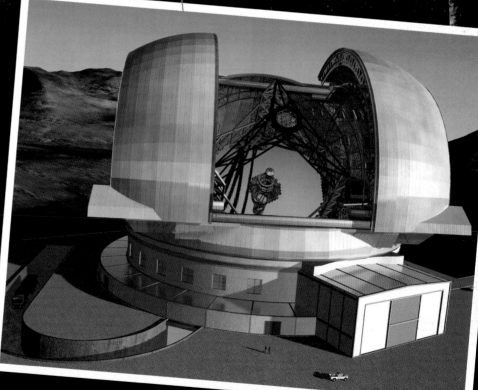

194

A new X-ray telescope is planned for launch in 2021. The International X-ray observatory will look at what happens near black holes and astronomers hope it will show black holes in young galaxies billions of years ago.

▲ The European Extremely Large Telescope will be the largest optical telescope in the world when it is built in the Atacama Desert in Chile.

EXPLORING SPACE

195 For thousands of years people gazed up at the night sky and wondered what it would be like to explore space. This became a reality around 50 years ago, and since then humans have been to the Moon, and unmanned spacecraft have visited all of the planets in the Solar System. Spacecraft have also explored other planets' moons, asteroids and glowing comets. These amazing discoveries help us to understand the Universe.

▶ ESA's *Integral* satellite (launched in 2002) is deployed from a Proton rocket to observe invisible gamma rays in space. Since 1957, humans have sent spacecraft to all eight planets in the Solar System, as well as more than 50 moons, asteroids and comets.

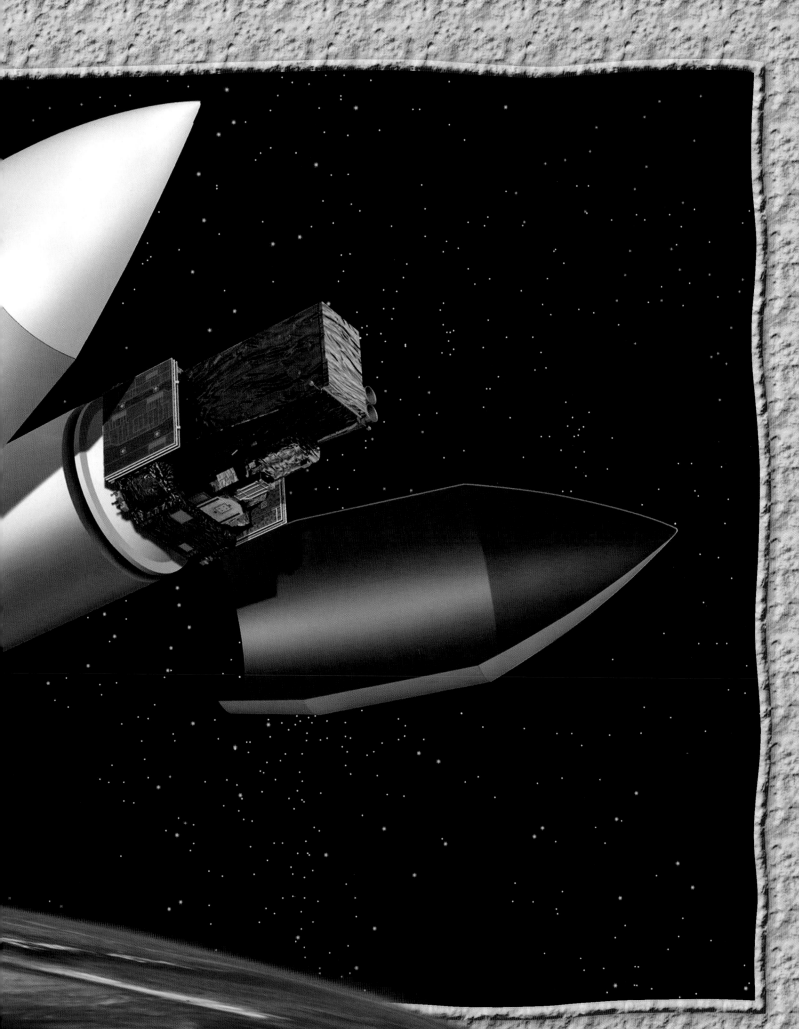

Who explores, and why?

196 Exploring space involves sending craft, robots, equipment and sometimes people to planets, moons, asteroids and comets. Some craft fly near to their targets, while others land. As they explore, they gather information to send back to Earth.

197 Space exploration is different from other space sciences. For example, astronomy is the study of objects in space including planets, stars and galaxies, as well as the Universe as a whole. Much of this is done using telescopes, rather than travelling out into space.

198 The *Cassini-Huygens* mission to Saturn is the most expensive mission ever. It cost more than $3.3 billion – the price of 12 Airbus A380 super jumbo jets.

Vandenberg Air Force Base and Spaceport, California, USA

NORTH AMERICA

NASA Headquarters, Washington D.C., USA

Kennedy Space, Center, Florida, USA

Alcantara Launch Center, Sao Luis, Brazil

Guiana Space Centre, Kourou, French Guiana

SOUTH AMERICA

▼ Astronomers use huge, extremely powerful telescopes to observe outer space from Earth.

▲ Space mission headquarters and launch sites are spread across the world.

199 Space exploration is complicated and expensive. Generally, only large nations, such as the USA, Russia, Japan and Europe, send craft into space. Recently, China and India have also launched exploratory missions.

200 Sending even a small spacecraft into space costs vast amounts of money. The Japanese *Hayabusa* mission to bring back samples of the comet Itokawa began in 2003. It lasted seven years and cost around $170 million. Sending the *Phoenix* lander to Mars in 2008 was even more expensive, at $450 million dollars.

▶ The comet-visiting *Hayabusa* spacecraft blasted off from Uchinoura Space Centre, Japan, in 2003. It returned to Earth in 2010, carrying samples of comet dust.

European Space Agency Headquarters, Paris, France

Roscomos Headquarters, Moscow, Russia

ASIA

EUROPE

Uchinoura Space Centre, Japan

Xichang Satellite Launch Center, China

Balkonur Cosmodrome (Russian), Kazakhstan

AFRICA

Tanegashima Space Center, Japan

Shar Space Launch Center, Sriharikota Island, India

▼ Recent observations in space suggest faraway stars could have planets forming around them from bits of gas, dust and rock – similiar to our own Solar System.

201 If the costs are so great, why do we explore space? Exploring the unknown has long been a part of human nature. Space exploration provides clues that may help us to understand how the Universe formed. Progress in space technology can also help advances on Earth.

Early explorers

202 The Space Age began in 1957 when Russia launched *Sputnik 1*, the first Earth-orbiting satellite. It was a metal, ball-shaped craft that could measure pressure and temperature, and send radio signals back to Earth.

▼ Tracking *Sputnik 1*'s orbit showed how the upper atmosphere of the Earth fades into space.

203 In 1958, the USA launched the satellite *Explorer 1*. As it orbited the Earth it detected two doughnut-shaped belts of high-energy particles, known as the Van Allen Belts. They can damage spacecraft and interfere with radio signals.

◄ The Van Allen belts are made up of particles, trapped by Earth's natural magnetic field.

Inner belt

Outer belt

Heat-resistant outer casing

Inner casing

204 In 1959, Russia's *Luna 1* spacecraft was aiming for the Moon, but it missed. Later that year, *Luna 2* crashed into the Moon on purpose, becoming the first craft to reach another world. On its way down the craft measured the Moon's gravity and magnetism.

Batteries

Antennae

Ventilation fan

QUIZ

Early exploration was a 'Space Race' between the USA and the Soviet Union. Which had these 'firsts'?

1. First satellite in space
2. First person in space
3. First craft on the Moon
4. First person on the Moon

Answers:
1, 2, 3 – Russia 4 – USA

Hatch

Heat shield
covering

Long range
antenna

◀ Gagarin's *Vostok I*
spacecraft was ten
times larger than the
Sputnik I satellite, and
50 times heavier.

Descent module –
only this ball-shaped
part came back
to Earth

Oxygen and nitrogen
gas tanks for fuel and
for Gagarin to breathe

Retro-thruster

205
**The first person in space was
Russian cosmonaut Yuri Gagarin.** In 1961 he made
one orbit of Earth in the spacecraft *Vostok 1*. The
furthest he travelled into space was 327 kilometres.
Gagarin's trip made news around the world and
showed that humans could survive in space.

206
**The US sent seven
Surveyor craft to the Moon
between 1966 and 1968.** Five
succeeded in soft-landing (landing
without being destroyed) on the surface.
This was an important stage in planning
the most exciting and ambitious mission
of all – sending people to another world.

▶ *Surveyor 3* landed on the Moon in
April 1967. It was photographed by the
Apollo 12 astronauts in November 1969.

Man on the Moon

207 The only humans to have explored another world are 12 US astronauts that were part of the Apollo program. Six Apollo missions landed on the Moon between 1969 and 1972, each with two astronauts. First to step onto the surface were Neil Armstrong and Buzz Aldrin from *Apollo 11*, on 20 July, 1969.

208 Each Apollo lunar lander touched down on a different type of terrain. The astronauts stayed on the Moon for three or four days. They explored, carried out experiments and collected samples of Moon dust and rocks to bring back to Earth.

209 The last three Apollo missions took a Lunar Roving Vehicle (LRV), or 'Moon buggy'. The astronauts drove for up to 20 kilometres at a time, exploring the Moon's hills, valleys, flat plains and cliffs.

210 Since the Apollo missions, more than 50 unmanned spacecraft have orbited or landed on the Moon. In 1994, US orbiter *Clementine* took many photographs, gravity readings and detailed maps of the Moon's surface.

◄ *Apollo 15*'s Lunar Module pilot James Irwin salutes the US flag and his Commander David Scott, in 1971. Their Lunar Module lander is behind and the Moon buggy is to the right.

MISSION	DATE	CREW	ACHIEVEMENT
Apollo 11	July 1969	Neil Armstrong (C) Buzz Aldrin (LMP) Michael Collins (CMP)	First humans on another world
Apollo 12	November 1969	Pete Conrad (C) Alan Bean (LMP) Richard Gordon (CMP)	First colour television pictures of the Moon returned to Earth
Apollo 13	April 1970	James Lovell (C) Fred Haise (LMP) Ken Mattingly (CMP)	Apollo 13 turned back after launch because of an explosion. It never reached the Moon, but returned safely to Earth
Apollo 14	January–February 1971	Alan Shepard (C) Edgar Mitchell (LMP) Stuart Roosa (CMP)	Longest Moon walks in much improved spacesuits
Apollo 15	July–August 1971	David Scott (C) James Irwin (LMP) Alfred Worden (CMP)	First use of a Moon buggy allowed astronauts to explore a wider range
Apollo 16	April 1972	John Young (C) Charles Duke (LMP) Thomas Mattingly (CMP)	First and only mission to land in the Moon's highlands
Apollo 17	December 1972	Eugene Cernan (C) Harrison Schmitt (LMP) Ronald Evans (CMP)	Returned a record 49 kilograms of rock and dust samples

211 In 2009, the *Lunar Reconnaissance Orbiter* began mapping the Moon's surface in detail. Its pictures showed parts of the Apollo craft left by the astronauts. In the same year the Indian orbiter *Chandrayaan 1* discovered ice on the Moon.

◄ On each mission, the Commander (C) and the Lunar Module pilot (LMP) landed on the Moon, while the Command Module pilot (CMP) stayed in the orbiting craft.

Plan and prepare

212 Planning a mission takes many years. Scientists suggest places to explore, what might be discovered, and the cost. Their government must agree for the mission to go ahead.

▲ In 1961 US space engineer John Houbolt developed the idea of using a three-part spacecraft for the Apollo Moon missions.

213 There are many types of exploratory missions. A flyby takes the spacecraft near to its target world, and past. An orbiter circles around the target. A lander mission touches down on the surface. A lander may release a rover, which can travel around on the surface.

▲ For worlds with an atmosphere, parachutes are used to lower a lander gently. This parachute design for a planned mission to Mars is being tested in the world's biggest wind tunnel in California, USA.

214 The ever-changing positions of Earth and other objects in space mean there is a limited 'launch window' for each mission. This is when Earth is in the best position for a craft to reach its target in the shortest time. If the launch window is missed, the distances may become too massive.

▼ The *New Horizons* spacecraft was assembled and checked in perfectly clean, dust-free conditions before being launched to Pluto in 2006.

215 In space, repairs are difficult or impossible. Exploring craft must be incredibly reliable, with tested and proven technology. Each piece of equipment needs a back-up, and even if this fails, it should not affect other parts.

216
A spacecraft must be able to cope with the conditions in space and on other worlds. It is incredibly cold in space, but planets such as Venus are hotter than boiling water. Other planets have hazards such as clouds made of tiny drops of acid.

▶ The spacecraft *Galileo* was tested in ultra-bright light of the same level that it would receive as it flew nearer the Sun in 1990 on its way to Jupiter.

217
A robot submarine called *Endurance* may one day explore oceans on distant planets or moons. It has been tested in frozen lakes in Antarctica and near-boiling pools in New Zealand.

218
A test version of the spacecraft is tried on Earth. If successful, the real craft is built in strict conditions. One loose screw or speck of dust could cause disaster. There's no second chance once the mission begins.

Blast off!

219 A spacecraft is blasted into space by its launch vehicle, or rocket. The rocket is the only machine powerful enough to reach 'escape velocity' – the speed needed to break free from the pull of Earth's gravity. Usually the spacecraft is folded up in the nose cone of the rocket.

220 Different sizes of rockets are used for different sizes of spacecraft. One of the heaviest was the *Cassini-Huygens* mission to Saturn. At its launch in 1997, with all its fuel and equipment on board, it weighed 5.6 tonnes – almost as much as a school bus. It needed a huge *Titan IV* rocket launcher to power it into space.

221 Spacecraft and other objects carried by the rocket are called the 'payload'. Most rockets take their payload into orbit around the Earth. The nose cone opens to release the craft stored inside. Parts of it unfold, such as the solar panels that turn sunlight into electricity.

Launch point

Escape velocity

Orbit bound by Earth's gravity

◀ Launch vehicles must quickly reach escape velocity – 11,200 metres per second – to shrug off Earth's gravitational pull.

SECOND STAGE (S-II)
The middle section of the launcher had five J-2 rocket engines. It was 25 metres tall, and like the first stage, was 10 metres wide.

FIRST STAGE (S-IC)
The bottom part of *Saturn V* was 42 metres tall. The F-1 rocket engines propelled the entire launch vehicle for the first 60 kilomentres.

F-1 rocket engines

J-2 rocket engines

▲ The biggest launchers were the three-stage *Saturn V* rockets used to launch the Apollo missions. Each stage fell away after using up its fuel.

▶ Europe's *Ariane 5* has one main rocket engine and two boosters. These boosters burn for the first 129 seconds, then detach.

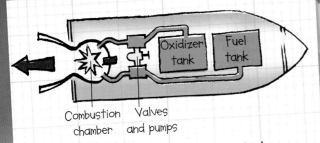

▲ Liquid-fuel rocket engines have a tank of liquid fuel and a tank of liquid oxygen or an oxygen-rich chemical. When the two mix together and ignite, they burn and create thrust.

THIRD STAGE (S-IVB)
The third stage was 17.8 metres tall and 6.6 metres wide. It had one J-2 engine (like those in the second stage).

Launch escape tower

Command Module

Service Module

Lunar Module

J-2 rocket engine

222 Craft are tested while in orbit around the Earth, to check the engines, radio communications, cameras and other parts are working. If there is a problem, a robot repair mission or some astronauts may be sent up. If everything is in working order, the craft can boost away from Earth to begin its long journey.

MAKE A ROCKET
You will need:
sheet of card   cardboard tube
sticky tape   scissors

Use the tube for the main body of the rocket. Make a cone shape with some of the card and stick it to one end. In a safe place, 'launch' the rocket by throwing it up at an angle. It should tumble out of control. Add fins by sticking four large, card triangles to the base. Now it should fly much straighter.

In deep space

223 Most spacecraft travel for months, even years, to their destinations. The fastest journey to Mars took just over six months, by *Mars Express* in 2003. *Pioneer 10* took 11 years to reach Neptune in 1983.

224 Launched in 2001, spacecraft *Deep Space 1* went on a trip to visit asteroids and comets. Its fuel tank was the size of a small suitcase, yet the fuel lasted for over three years.

◄ *Mars Express* cruised at a speed of 10,800 kilometres an hour on its way to Mars.

225 Guiding the craft on its course is vital. A tiny error could mean that it misses its distant target by millions of kilometres. Mission controllers on Earth regularly check the craft's position with radio signals using the Deep Space Network (DSN). The DSN is made up of three huge radio dishes located in California, USA, Madrid in Spain, and Canberra, Australia.

▼ This ion thruster is being tested in a vacuum chamber. The blue glow is the beam of charged atoms being thrown out of the engine.

226 Spacecraft only need small engines because there is no air in space to slow them down. Depending on the length of the journey, different kinds of engines and fuels are used. The ion thruster uses magnetism made by electricity. This hurls tiny particles, called ions, backwards, which pushes the craft forwards.

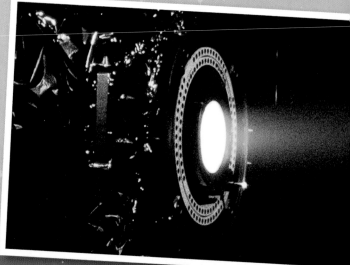

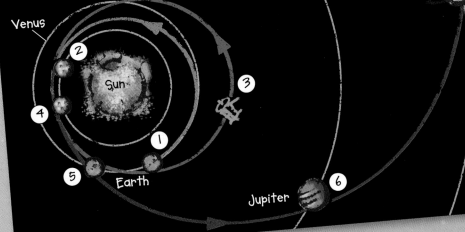

Venus

Saturn

2

Sun

3

4

1

5

Earth

6

Jupiter

◄ Bowl-shaped antennae (aerials), like *New Horizons*', exchange radio signals to and from Earth.

227
Craft often pass other planets or moons on their journeys. Like Earth, these objects all have a gravitational pull, and this could send a craft off course. However, a planet's gravity may be used to propel the craft in a new direction to save fuel. This is known as a gravity-assisted flyby or 'slingshot'.

▲ *Cassini-Huygens*' journey to Saturn involved four gravity-assists. The main stages were: launch to first Venus flyby (orange), second Venus flyby (blue), and Earth flyby, past Jupiter to Saturn (purple).

KEY

1 October 1997 Launch from Earth

2 April 1998 First Venus flyby

3 December 1998 Engine fires for 90 minutes to return to Venus

4 June 1999 Second Venus flyby

5 August 1999 Earth–Moon flyby

6 December 2000 Jupiter flyby

7 July 2004 Arrives in orbit around Saturn

Goldstone, California, USA

◄▼ The three Deep Space Network sites are equally spaced around Earth, with 120 degrees between them, making a 360-degree circle.

Madrid, Spain

Canberra Australia

► The Deep Space Network's radio dish at Goldstone near Barstow, California, is 70 metres across.

228
For long periods, much of a craft's equipment shuts down to save electricity. It's like an animal hibernating in winter or a mobile phone on stand-by. When the craft 'hibernates' only a few vital systems stay active, such as navigation.

Ready to explore

229 As the spacecraft approaches its target, its systems power up and it 'comes to life'. Controllers on Earth test the craft's radio communications and other equipment. At such enormous distances, radio signals can take minutes, even hours, to make the journey.

230 Among the most important devices onboard a craft are cameras. Some work like telescopes to take a close-up or magnified view of a small area. Others are wide-angle cameras, which capture a much greater area without magnifying.

231 Other kinds of camera can 'see' types of waves that are invisible to the human eye. These include infrared or heat rays, ultraviolet rays, radio waves and X-rays. These rays and waves provide information about the target world, such as how hot or cold it is.

▼ *Mars Reconnaissance Orbiter's* photograph of the 730-metre-wide Victoria Crater was captured by its high-resolution camera and shows amazing detail.

The Mars Climate Sounder records the temperature, moisture and dust in the Martian atmosphere

The high-resolution camera captures close-up, detailed photographs of the surface

QUIZ

Spacecraft have many devices, but rarely microphones to detect sound. Why?
A. The chance of meeting aliens who can shout loudly is very small.
B. Sound waves do not travel through the vacuum of space.
C. It's too difficult to change sound waves into radio signals.

Answer: B

98

Antenna

232 Magnetometers detect magnetic fields, which exist naturally around some planets, including Earth. Gravitometers measure the target object's pull of gravity. This is especially important in the final stage of the journey – the landing. Some spacecraft also have space dust collectors.

Solar panel

◄ *Mars Reconnaissance Orbiter*, launched in 2005, carries a telescopic camera, wide-angle cameras, sensors for infrared and ultraviolet light and a radar that 'sees' below the surface.

The spectrometer identifies different substances on the surface by measuring how much light is reflected

233 The information from the cameras and sensors is turned into radio signal codes and beamed back to Earth. To send and receive these signals, the craft has one or more dish-shaped antennae. These must be in the correct position to communicate with the dishes located on Earth.

The sub-surface radar can see up to one kilometre below the planet's surface

Flyby, bye-bye

234 On a flyby mission, a spacecraft comes close to its target. It does not go into orbit around it or land – it flies onwards and away into deep space. Some flybys are part of longer missions to even more distant destinations. In these cases the flyby may also involve gravity assist.

LAUNCH FROM EARTH
20 August, 1977

235 A flyby craft may pass its target several times on a long, lop-sided path, before leaving again. Each pass gives a different view of the target object. The craft's cameras, sensors and other equipment switch on to take pictures and record measurements, then turn off again as it flies away.

JUPITER

Flyby on 9 July, 1979

236 The ultimate flyby craft was *Voyager 2*. It made a 'Grand Tour' of the four outermost planets, which are only suitably aligned every 175 years. *Voyager 2* blasted off in 1977 and flew past Jupiter in 1979, Saturn in 1981, Uranus in 1986 and Neptune in 1989. This craft is still sending back information from a distance twice as far as Pluto is from Earth.

I DON'T BELIEVE IT!

When *Pioneer 11* zoomed to within 43,000 kilometres of Jupiter in 1974, it made the fastest-ever flyby at 50 kilometres per second.

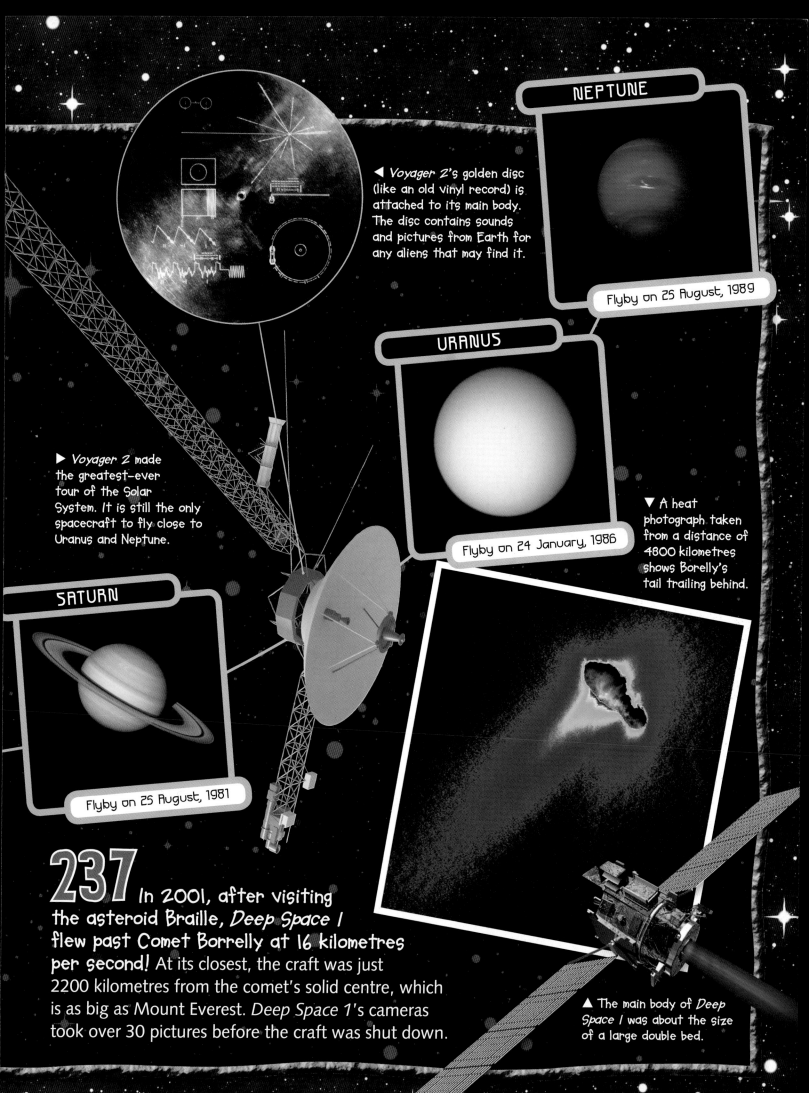

◀ *Voyager 2*'s golden disc (like an old vinyl record) is attached to its main body. The disc contains sounds and pictures from Earth for any aliens that may find it.

Flyby on 25 August, 1989

URANUS

▶ *Voyager 2* made the greatest-ever tour of the Solar System. It is still the only spacecraft to fly close to Uranus and Neptune.

▼ A heat photograph taken from a distance of 4800 kilometres shows Borelly's tail trailing behind.

Flyby on 24 January, 1986

SATURN

Flyby on 25 August, 1981

237 In 2001, after visiting the asteroid Braille, *Deep Space 1* flew past Comet Borrelly at 16 kilometres per second! At its closest, the craft was just 2200 kilometres from the comet's solid centre, which is as big as Mount Everest. *Deep Space 1*'s cameras took over 30 pictures before the craft was shut down.

▲ The main body of *Deep Space 1* was about the size of a large double bed.

Into orbit

238 On many exploring missions the craft is designed to go into orbit around its target world. Craft that do this are called orbiters, and they provide a much longer, closer look than a flyby mission.

▶ There are several different types of orbit that craft can make around their targets. Here, they are shown around Earth.

A polar orbit passes over the North and South Poles

An equatorial orbit goes around the middle (Equator)

Most orbits are elliptical, with low and high points

239 One of the most elliptical orbits was made by *Mars Global Surveyor*. At its closest, it passed Mars at a distance of 171 kilometres, twice in each orbit. The craft's furthest distance away was more than ten times greater.

◀ In 2006, two twin STEREO-craft went into orbit around the Sun. With one in front and one behind Earth, the craft made the first 3D observations of the Sun.

Antenna

ORBITER

You will need:
sock   tennis ball   string (one metre long)

Put the ball in the sock and tie up the top with the string. Go outside. Holding the string half way along its length, whirl the sock above your head so that it 'orbits' you. Gradually lengthen the string – does the 'orbit' take longer?

DIONE

240 The *Cassini* orbiter, part of the *Cassini-Huygens* mission, has been through many changes of orbit around Saturn. Some went close to the main planet and some passed near to its rings. Other orbits took it past Saturn's largest moon, Titan, and its smaller moons, including Enceladus, Iapetus and Mimas.

During its orbits of Saturn, *Cassini* passed Dione, Saturn's 15th largest moon. Saturn can be seen in the distance.

241 A spacecraft's radar checks its average height above the surface. Radio or microwave signals beam down to the surface and bounce back. The time this takes tells the craft how far away it is. More detailed radar measurements map the surface far below.

Camera

242 A spectrometer analyzes different colours in light waves. Different chemical substances give off or reflect certain colours of light better than others. By reading this, the spectrometer can work out what substances are present in a planet's atmosphere or on its surface.

▶ *Mars Global Surveyor*'s average orbital height was 378 kilometres. It mapped the entire Martian surface.

Solar panel

243 The orbiter continually checks and adjusts its height and position. It does this using tiny puffs of gas from its thrusters, which stops the craft losing speed and crashing into the surface.

Landers and impactors

244 Some missions have landers that touch down onto the surface of their target world. Part of the spacecraft may detach and land while the other part stays in orbit, or the whole spacecraft may land.

① Spacecraft in orbit

② Landing module separates from orbiter

③ First parachute opened, then detached

▶ The later landers of the Russian *Venera* program (1961–1983) used parachutes to slow down in the thick, hot, cloudy atmosphere of Venus.

245 The journey down can be hazardous. If the planet has an atmosphere (layer of gas around it) there may be strong winds that could blow the lander off course. If the atmosphere is thick, there may be huge pressure pushing on the craft.

④ Main parachutes opened at a height of 50 kilometres above the surface

⑤ Ring-shaped shock absorber filled with compressed gas lessened the impact at touchdown

246 If there is an atmosphere, the lander may use parachutes, or inflate its own balloons or air bags, to slow its speed. On the *Cassini-Huygens* mission, the *Huygens* lander used two parachutes as it descended for touchdown on Saturn's moon, Titan.

247 If there is no atmosphere, retro-thrusters are used to slow the craft down. These puff gases in the direction of travel. Most landers have a strong, bouncy casing for protection as they hit the surface, or long, springy legs to reduce the impact.

▲ A photograph taken by *Deep Impact* 67 seconds after its impactor crashed into Comet Tempel 1, shows material being thrown out.

▲ This image shows how *Beagle 2*'s solar panels were designed to fold out. However contact with the lander was lost soon after it detached from its orbiter in 2003.

248
After touchdown, the lander's solar panels and other parts fold out. Its equipment and systems switch on, and it tests its radio communications with the orbiter and sometimes directly with Earth.

Impactor

249
Some craft are designed to smash into their target, and these are called impactors. The crash is observed by the orbiter and may also be watched by controllers on Earth. The dust, rocks and gases given off by an impact provide valuable information about the target object.

Camera

▶ In 2005, *Deep Impact* released its impactor, watched it strike Comet Tempel 1 and studied the resulting crater.

◀ *Mars Pathfinder* lander being tested on Earth. It used a parachute, retro-thrusters and multi-bubble air bags to land on Mars.

Robotic rovers

250 After touchdown, some landers release small, robotic vehicles called rovers. They have wheels and motors so they can move around on the surface to explore. So far rovers have explored on the Moon and Mars.

Antennae

Laser reflector

Solar panels

Cameras

Wheels

▶ In the 1970s, Russia sent two rovers, *Lunokhod 1* and *2*, to the Moon. Each was the size of a large bathtub, weighed almost one tonne and had eight wheels driven by electric motors.

251 Modern rovers are mostly robotic — self-controlled using onboard computers. This is because of the time delay of radio signals. Even when Earth and Mars are at their closest distance to each other, radio signals take over three minutes to travel one way. If a rover was driven by remote control from Earth, it could have fallen off a cliff long before its onboard cameras relayed images of this.

252 Rovers are designed and tested to survive the conditions on their target world. Scientists know about these conditions from information collected from observations on Earth, and from previous missions. Test rovers are driven on extreme landscapes on Earth to make sure they can handle tricky terrain.

▲ A test version of a new rover destined for Mars, here being tested on the slippery rocks of a beach in Wales, UK.

253 The *Spirit* and *Opportunity* rovers landed on Mars in 2004. They are equipped with cameras that allow them to navigate around obstacles. Heat-sensitive cameras detect levels of heat soaked up by rocks, giving clues to what the rocks are made of. On-board microscopes and magnets gather and study dust particles containing iron.

Navcam

Antenna

Main antenna

Solar panels

▶ Twin rovers *Spirit* and *Opportunity* are each about the size of an office desk.

Mobile arm carries five gadgets including a camera, rock grinder and magnets

Each wheel has an electric motor

254 A rover for Venus is planned, but its surface temperature is over 400°C. Plastics and some metals would melt there. A Venus rover would have to be made out of metals such as titanium, which have high melting points. Its inner workings would need to be continually cooled.

Close-up look

▶ In the late 1970s the USA's two Viking landers photographed their robotic sampler arms digging into Mars' surface.

255 Some landers and rovers have robot arms that extend from the main body. These scoop or drill into the surface to collect samples, which are then tested in the craft's onboard science laboratory. Samples are tested for chemical reactions, such as bubbling or changing colour.

Solar panel

Robotic arm with scoop and camera

Spheres of minerals containing iron, known as 'blueberries'

Circular area ground by tool is 4.5 centimetres across

256 Most rovers have six wheels. This design allows them to move quickly around sharp corners, without tipping over. Each wheel has an electric motor, powered by onboard batteries that are charged by the solar panels. If the batteries run down, the rover 'sleeps' until light from the Sun recharges them.

◀ Mars rovers *Spirit* and *Opportunity* are both equipped with a rock-grinding tool. They use it to grind into rocks and gather dust samples.

257

The *Phoenix* Mars lander had several devices on its robotic arm to measure features of Martian soil. It measured how easily it carried (conducted) heat and electricity, and if it contained any liquids. *Phoenix* also had microscopes for an ultra-close view of the surface samples.

Meteorological (weather) station

Gas analyzers

Mini science laboratory

Solar panel

258

One type of rover drill uses heat to melt or burn a hole, which could be useful on icy planets. A thermal rover could even melt its way through ice, perhaps to water beneath, to look for alien life.

259

Most landers and rovers have mini weather stations. Sensors measure temperatures and pressures through the day and night and record the Sun's brightness. They also take samples of gases if there is an atmosphere, and record weather, such as wind and dust storms.

◄ The *Phoenix* Mars lander of 2008 had a robotic arm, on the left, and a small weather station.

260

The orbiting craft acts as a relay station to receive signals from its lander and send them on to Earth. A lander can in turn be a relay station for a rover. A rover has a small radio set to communicate with the lander and the lander has a slightly larger one to communicate with the orbiter. The orbiter has the biggest radio set to communicate with Earth.

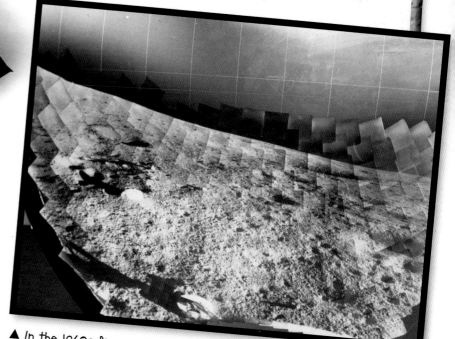

▲ In the 1960s five US Surveyor landers sent back separate close-up photographs of the Moon's surface. These were joined together to make larger scenes.

Exploring Mars

JUL 1965 *Mariner 4* flew past Mars and took the first close-up photos of another planet

261 Mars is the nearest planet to Earth and the most explored. In the 1870s, astronomers thought they could see canals of water on Mars' surface, thought to be built by aliens. But with better telescopes, these 'canals' were found to be simply a trick of the light.

▼ This timeline shows some of the most notable missions in the exploration of Mars.

NOV 1971 *Mariner 9* entered orbit around Mars – the first craft to orbit another planet

DEC 1971 *Mars 3*'s lander was the first to touch down safely on Mars, but contact was lost after 20 seconds

262 Since the 1960s more than 40 missions have set off to Mars. About two-thirds of them failed at launch or on the way. One-quarter have failed at or near Mars, leading some people to believe that Martians were attacking and destroying the craft.

JUL/SEP 1976 *Viking 1 and 2* were the first successful landers on the surface of Mars

JUL 1997 *Mars Pathfinder* landed and released *Sojourner*, the first rover, on another planet

◄ *Mars Odyssey* (2001) produced this image of Mars' south pole. The Martian polar ice caps are made of frozen water and 'dry ice' – solid (frozen) carbon dioxide.

263 In 1976, two US Viking landers carried out research on Mars. They took many photographs, made detailed maps and tested the atmosphere, rocks and soil, but they found no definite signs of life. In 2008, the US *Phoenix* lander discovered water frozen as ice, and many minerals and chemicals in the soil.

264 The *Spirit* and *Opportunity* rovers have made an amazing series of explorations and discoveries. They have found evidence that there was once water on Mars, and that it is possibly still there underground. In 2009 *Spirit* got stuck in soft soil but *Opportunity* is still moving, although very slowly.

MAY 2008 *Phoenix* lander touched down. It was the first craft to land in Mars' polar area

DEC 2003 In orbit, *Mars Express* released its lander, *Beagle 2*, but communications to it were lost

SEP 1997 *Mars Global Surveyor* went into orbit and began detailed, large-scale mapping of the surface

MAR 2006 *Mars Reconnaissance Orbiter* arrived, making a record six working craft in orbit or on the surface of Mars

265 The *Mars Science Laboratory* rover *Curiosity*, which landed in 2012, has a drill, scoop arm and several packages of experiments. It is the biggest-ever rover at almost one tonne in weight. Its aim is to find out if there is, or ever has been, any life on Mars.

JAN 2004 *Mars Exploration Rovers Spirit* and *Opportunity* arrived on the surface, ready to explore

◀ *Curiosity* is about the size of a Mini car and has a top speed of 2.5 centimetres per second.

Back on Earth

266
All spacecraft have a mission control centre on Earth. Expert teams monitor a craft's systems, including radio communications, and the data a craft collects from its cameras and instruments.

▲ Mission controllers at NASA's Jet Propulsion Laboratory in California, USA, celebrate as the first images from rover *Opportunity* reach Earth.

267
Missions often run into problems. Controllers must work out how to keep a mission going when faults occur. If power supplies fail, the teams may have to decide to switch off some equipment so that others can continue working.

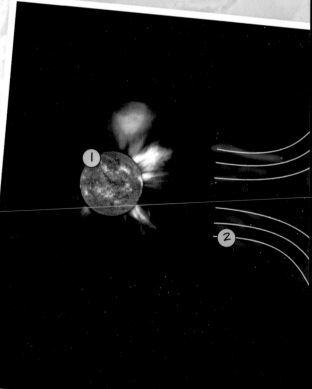

268
Sample return missions bring items from space back to Earth. In 2004, the *Genesis* craft dropped off its return container. It was supposed to parachute down to Earth's surface, but it crash-landed in Utah, USA. Luckily, some of its samples of solar wind survived for study.

269
Gases, dust, rocks and other items are brought back to Earth to be studied. In the early 1970s the six manned Apollo missions brought a total of 381.7 kilograms of Moon material back to Earth.

▲ This piece of basalt Moon rock, brought back by *Apollo 15*, is being studied by *Apollo 17* astronaut and geologist (rock expert) Jack Schmitt.

270
Samples returned from space must not be contaminated with material from Earth. Keeping samples clean allows scientists to find out what they contain, and stops any dangerous substances being released on Earth. Spacecraft are ultra-clean at launch to prevent them spreading chemicals or germs from Earth to other worlds.

▼ *Genesis* collected high-energy particles from the Sun's solar wind, which distorts Earth's magnetic field.

I DON'T BELIEVE IT!

Moon rocks don't look very special, yet over 100 small ones brought back by the Apollo missions have been stolen. More than ten people have been caught trying to sell them.

▶ This sample of Moon rock collected during the *Apollo 11* mission is housed inside a securely fastened, airtight container.

KEY
1. Sun
2. Solar wind
3. Bow shock (where the solar wind meets Earth's magnetic field)
4. Earth's magnetic field
5. Earth

This photograph taken by *SOHO* uses a disc with a hole to block out some of the Sun's glare. This reveals vast streaming clouds of superheated matter called plasma.

Corona

Coronal mass ejection (CME) of superhea...

271
Missions to the Sun encounter enormous heat. In the 1970s the US-German craft *Helios 2* flew to within 44 million kilometres of the Sun. From 1990, the *Ulysses* probe travelled on a huge orbit, passing near the Sun and as far out as Jupiter.

272
In 1996, the *SOHO* satellite began studying the Sun from near Earth. Since then, it has found many new comets. In 2015, *Solar Probe Plus* will orbit to within six million kilometres of the Sun, with a shield-like 'sunshade' of heat-resistant, carbon-composite material for protection.

◀ The Helios mission was featured on stamps worldwide.

1c

HELIOS MISSION

GRENADA

▲ *Messenger* had a 'sunshade' made out of a ceramic-composite material to protect it from the Sun's heat.

274
Mercury, the nearest planet to the Sun, has been visited by two spacecraft, *Mariner 10* in 1974, and *Messenger* in 2004. *Messenger* made flybys in 2008 and 2009 and is due in orbit in 2011. These craft measured Mercury's surface temperature at 420°C – twice as hot as a home oven.

273
Missions to Venus include Russia's Venera series (1961 to 1984), US Mariner probes (1962 to 1973) and *Pioneer Venus* (1978). From 1990 to 1994, *Magellan* used a radar to map the surface in amazing detail. In 2006, Europe's *Venus Express* began more mapping. Its instruments also studied Venus' extreme global warming.

275
More than 20 craft have visited Venus, the second planet from the Sun. Its atmosphere of thick clouds, extreme pressures, temperatures over 450°C and acid chemicals, pose huge challenges for exploring craft.

◀ Studying Venus' atmosphere may help us understand similar climate processes happening on Earth.

Antenna

Solar panel

Positioning thrusters

Main rocket engine

Gold coating helps to keep out the Sun's heat

▲ *Venus Express* orbits as low as 250 kilometres above the poles of Venus.

276
The fastest spacecraft, and the fastest man-made object ever, was *Helios 2*. It neared the Sun at 67 kilometres per second!

277 Asteroids orbit the Sun but are far smaller than planets, so even finding them is a challenge. Most large asteroids are in the main asteroid belt between Mars and Jupiter. Much closer to us are near-Earth Asteroids (NEAs), and more than 20 have been explored in detail by flyby craft, orbiters and landers.

Mars

Ceres

Vesta

Pallas

Hygiea

278 Orbiting and landing on asteroids is very difficult. Many asteroids are oddly shaped, and they roll and tumble as they move through space. A craft may only discover this as it gets close.

◄ Dwarf planet Ceres and the three largest asteroids in our Solar System, seen against North America for scale. Vesta, the biggest asteroid, is about 530 kilometres across.

279 In 1996, the probe NEAR–Shoemaker launched towards NEA Eros. On the way it flew past asteroid Mathilde in the main belt. Then in 2000 it orbited 34-kilometre-long Eros, before landing. The probe discovered that the asteroid was peanut-shaped, and also gathered information about Eros' rocks, magnetism and movement. In 2008, spacecraft *Rosetta* passed main belt asteroid Steins, and asteroid Lutetia in 2010.

Jupiter

▲ In the main belt there are some dense 'asteroid swarms'. But most larger asteroids are tens of thousands of kilometres apart.

280 In 2010 Japan's *Hayabusa* brought back samples of asteroid Itokawa after touching down on its surface in 2005. This information has helped our understanding of asteroids as 'leftovers' from the formation of the Solar System 4600 million years ago.

281 *Dawn* was launched in 2007, to explore Vesta – the biggest asteroid – in 2011 and the dwarf planet Ceres in 2015. Vesta may be rocky, while Ceres is thought to be icier, with various chemicals frozen as solids. *Dawn* aims to find out for sure.

▲ The *Dawn* mission badge shows its two main targets.

▶ *Hayabusa* was designed to gather samples of the asteroid Itokawa by firing a metal pellet towards the surface. It could then collect the dust thrown up by the impact.

Comet mysteries

282 Comets travel to and from the edges of the Solar System and beyond as they orbit the Sun. Unlike long-period comets, which may take thousands of years to orbit, short-period comets orbit every 200 years or less and so can be explored.

▶ The Oort cloud surrounds the Solar System and is made up of icy objects. It may be the source of some Sun-orbiting comets.

Sun

Kuiper belt

▶ The Kuiper belt lies beyond Neptune's orbit and is about twice the size of the Solar System. It consists of lots of comet-like objects.

Neptune

283 Like asteroids, comets are difficult to find. Comets warm up and glow only as they near the Sun. Their tails are millions of kilometres long, but consist only of faint gases and dust. The centre, or nucleus, of a comet may give off powerful jets of dust and gases that could blow a craft off course.

▶ A typical comet is mostly dust and ice. It has a glowing area, or coma, around it, and a long tail that points away from the Sun.

Solid rock core

Nucleus is often only a few kilometres across

Jets of gas and dust escape as ice melts

Glowing cloud, or coma, around nucleus is illuminated by sunlight

Dust and ice surrounds core

284
The famous Halley's Comet last appeared in 1986. Several exploring craft, known as the 'Halley Armada', went to visit it. This included Europe's *Giotto* probe, which flew to within 600 kilometres of the comet's nucleus. There were also two Russian-French Vega probes, and *Sakigake* and *Suisei* from Japan.

▶ *Stardust* collected comet dust using a very lightweight foam, called aerogel, in a collector shaped like a tennis bat. The collector folded into the craft's bowl-like capsule for return to Earth.

285
In 2008, the *Stardust* probe returned a capsule of dust collected from the comet Wild 2. In 2005, *Deep Impact* visited Comet Tempel 1 and released an impactor to crash into its nucleus and study the dust and gases given off. These craft increase our knowledge of comets as frozen balls of icy chemicals, rock and dust.

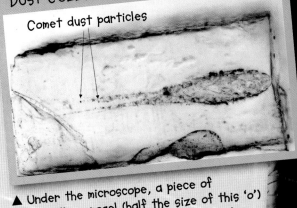

DUST COLLECTED FROM COMET WILD 2

Comet dust particles

▲ Under the microscope, a piece of *Stardust*'s aerogel (half the size of this 'o') is revealed to have minute dust particles embedded within it.

STARDUST APPROACHING COMET WILD 2

Glowing dust tail illuminated by sunlight

Ion (gas) tail appears bluish

SAMPLE CAPSULE RETURNS TO EARTH

Gas giants

286 The four furthest planets from Earth – Jupiter, Saturn, Uranus and Neptune – are 'gas giants'. These are large planets composed mainly of gases. It takes at least two years to reach Jupiter by the most direct route. But craft usually take longer because they use gravity assist.

▼ *Galileo* orbited Jupiter for more than seven years. It released an atmosphere probe to study the gases that make up almost the whole planet.

287 Craft entering Neptune's atmosphere would be hit by the fastest winds in the Solar System. These are ten times stronger than a hurricane on Earth!

288 There have been seven flybys of Jupiter and each one discovered more of the planet's moons. The two US Voyager missions, launched in 1977, discovered that Jupiter has rings like Saturn. US spacecraft *Galileo* arrived in orbit around Jupiter in 1995 and released a probe into the planet's atmosphere.

ON TITAN'S SURFACE

▲ *Huygens'* pictures from the surface of Titan, Saturn's largest moon, show lumps of ice and a haze of deadly methane gas.

289
The ringed planet Saturn had flybys by *Pioneer II* (1979) and *Voyagers I* and *2* (1980–1981). In 2004 the huge *Cassini-Huygens* craft arrived after a seven-year journey. The orbiter *Cassini* is still taking spectacular photographs of the planet, its rings and its moons.

▼ The *Huygens* lander separated from *Cassini* and headed for Titan. It sent back more than 750 images from the surface.

TITAN

290
The only exploring craft to have visited Uranus and Neptune is *Voyager 2*. During its flyby of Uranus in 1986, *Voyager 2* discovered ten new moons and two new rings. In 1989, the craft passed the outermost planet, Neptune, and discovered six new moons and four new rings.

A heat shield prevented burn-up on entry

Parachutes slowed the lander's descent

Huygens lands on Titan

▼ The four gas giants have many moons — some large, and some very small. This list includes the five largest moons for each (not to scale).

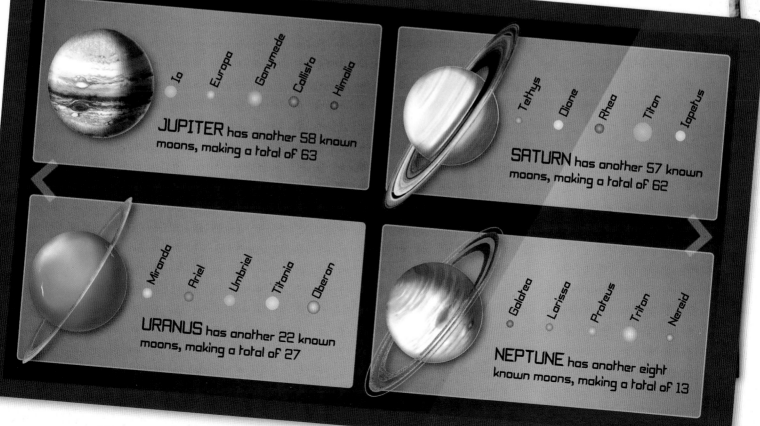

Io   Europa   Ganymede   Callisto   Himalia

JUPITER has another 58 known moons, making a total of 63

Tethys   Dione   Rhea   Titan   Iapetus

SATURN has another 57 known moons, making a total of 62

Miranda   Ariel   Umbriel   Titania   Oberon

URANUS has another 22 known moons, making a total of 27

Galatea   Larissa   Proteus   Triton   Nereid

NEPTUNE has another eight known moons, making a total of 13

Into the future

291 Sending craft to the edges of the Solar System takes many years. US spacecraft *NewHorizons* was launched in 2006, and is now heading for dwarf planet Pluto. The craft is due to reach Pluto in 2015 and may continue into the Kuiper Belt, the home of comets and more dwarf planets.

292 *New Horizons'* immense nine-year journey was complicated to plan. It includes a flyby of tiny asteroid 132534 APL, then a swing around Jupiter for gravity assist and a speed boost. Flybys of Jupiter's moons are also planned, before the long cruise to tiny Pluto. Without Jupiter's gravity assist, the trip would be five years longer.

◄ *New Horizons'* dish-shaped antenna is as big as a double bed. The grey, finned cylinder to the left is a tiny nuclear generator for electricity – solar panels are useless so far away from the Sun.

293

Several major explorations are planned for the coming years. The *ExoMars* mission consists of a lander and a rover, due to launch in 2016 and 2018. They will look for signs of life on Mars, using a 2-metre-deep drill. The *BepiColombo* mission aims to orbit Mercury and measure the Sun's power.

◀ The *BepiColombo* mission is planned for launch in 2014. The six-year trip will take the craft past the Moon, Earth and Venus before reaching Mercury — the closest planet to the Sun.

Drill

▲ The drill on *ExoMars* rover will pass soil samples to the mini laboratory on board for analysis.

294

What happens to exploring spacecraft? Some are deliberately crashed into other worlds, so that the impact can be observed by other spacecraft or from Earth. Others burn up as they enter the atmosphere of a planet or large moon.

295

Many exploring spacecraft are still travelling in space, and will be for thousands of years. As they run out of power they become silent, either sitting on their target worlds or drifting though empty space – unless they crash into an object. The most distant craft is *Voyager 1*, launched in 1977. It is now more than 17 billion kilometres from Earth, and is still being tracked.

▶ The 'Pale Blue Dot' photograph captured in 1990 by *Voyager 1*, was taken from six billion kilometres away. Earth is the tiny speck.

FAR-AWAY EARTH

Earth

Space magic and myth

▲ H G Wells' original story is brought to life in the 1953 movie *War of the Worlds*, in which martians invade Earth and destroy city after city. Humans can't stop them, but instead, germs eventually wipe out the alien invaders.

296 Exploring space has long been a favourite subject for story-telling. Even before rockets, there were theories about space travel and aliens. One of the first was *War of the Worlds*, written in 1898 by H G Wells.

◀ The mission statement of *Star Trek*'s starship *Enterprise* was: 'To explore strange new worlds, to seek out new life and new civilizations, to boldly go where no one has gone before.'

297 In the 1950s, as humans began to explore space, tales of sightings of 'flying saucers' and UFOs (Unidentified Flying Objects) soared. Some of these may be explained by secret aircraft or spacecraft being tested by governments. A few people claimed that aliens visited Earth and left signs, such as strange patterns in fields called crop circles.

298 The *Star Wars* (1977 onwards) and *Alien* movies (1979–2007) are all about adventures in space. This genre grew in popularity at the same time that space exploration was becoming a reality. The *Star Trek* movies (1979 onwards) had several spin-off television series, including *Voyager* and *Deep Space Nine*.

299 In the future, scientists may discover a form of ultra-fast travel involving black holes and wormholes (tunnels through space and time). This could allow humans to travel to distant galaxies to look for other 'Goldilocks' planets similar to Earth. Like the third bowl of porridge in the nursery story, the conditions on a Goldilocks planet are not too hot and not too cold, but 'just right' for life to exist. As yet, no others have been discovered.

QUIZ

1. What was the name of the story written by H G Wells about an alien invasion of Earth?
2. What does UFO stand for?
3. What is a 'Goldilocks' planet?

Answers:
1. *War of the Worlds*
2. Unidentified Flying Object
3. A planet that has the perfect conditions for life to exist – not too hot, not too cold, but 'just right'

300 Space scientists have suggested new kinds of rockets and thrusters for faster space travel. These could reduce the journey time to the next-nearest star, Proxima Centauri, to about 100 years. But one day we may be beaten to it – aliens from a distant galaxy could be exploring space right now and discover us first!

▼ Virgin Galactic will soon be offering space travel to the general public. A ticket for a flight on *SpaceShipTwo* (below) will cost $200,000!

N339SS

Index

126

ACKNOWLEDGEMENTS

The publishers would like to thank the following sources for the use of their photographs:

Key: t = top, b = bottom, l = left, r = right, c = centre, bg = background

Cover Illustration Peter Bull Art Studio
Alamy 107(tr) Keith Morris
Corbis 51(c) Araldo de Luca; 65(tl) IAC/GTC 91 Roger Ressmeye; 103(t) Michael Benson/Kinetikon Pictures; 112(t) Bill Ingalls/NASA/ Handout/CNP; 113(t) Roger Ressmeyer
Digital Vision 32(bl); 44(tr)
Dreamstime 60(c) Kramer-1; 68(t) Silverstore
European Space Agency 96(r) D. Ducros; 111Mars Express D. Ducros; 112–113(b); 115(bl) 2007 MPS/DLR-PF/IDA; 121(tl) ESA/NASA/JPL/ University of Arizona; 123(t) C. Carreau, (tr) AOES Medialab
Fotolia.com 57(tl) Georgios Kollidas, (r) Konstantin Sutyagin; 60(tc) pdtnc; 60–61(bg) Jenny Solomon; 80(clockwise from bl) Stephen Coburn, Petar Ishmeriev, pelvidge, Mats Tooming; 86(bl) Daniel
Getty 109(br) Time & Life Pictures; 108–109(bg) SSPL via Getty Images; 120 Time & Life Pictures
iStockphoto.com 13(b) 101cats; 56–57(bg) Duncan Walker; 57(br) Steven Wynn; 58(cr) Steven Wynn; 59(br) Steven Wynn; 60(tl) HultonArchive; 61(tc) Duncan Walker; 92–93(bg) Nicholas Belton; 100(r) Jan Rysavy
NASA Images 5(b), 5(r); 8(tl), (bl), (bc); 9(cl) The Exploratorium; 13(tr), (br) JPL-Caltech; 14(tr) JPL/USGS, 14(b) JPL; 15(tr), (bl); 16(br) Johns Hopkins University Applied Physics Laboratory/Carnegie Institution of Washington; 18(c) JPL/University of Arizona, (bl), (br); 19(tr) JPL/Space Science Institute, (bl) E. Karkoschka (University of Arizona); 20(tl) ESA, and L. Lamy (Observatory of Paris, CNRS, CNES), (br) H. Richer (University of British Columbia); 27 (tr) JPL-Caltech/STScI/CXC/SAO, 21(cl); 25(tr) ESA/STScI; 26(tr), (bl) ESA, K. Noll (STScI), (br) NASA/CXC; 29(tr), (tl) CXC/KIPAC/S.Allen et al; Radio: NRAO/ VLA/G.Taylor; Infrared: NASA/ESA/McMaster Univ./W.Harris; (cl) ESA, and the Hubble Heritage (STScI/AURA)-ESA/Hubble Collaboration, (bl) ESA, A. Nota (ESA/STScI/AURA); 30(bl) ESA, M. Livio (STScI) and the Hubble Heritage Team (STScI/AURA); (cr);; 33(l), (m) Dick Clark; 34(tr); 35(b); 37(tr); 39(tr); 40(t); 43(m); 44(l); 48(bl) GReatest Images of NASA (NASA-HQ-GRIN), (br) NASA Goddard Space Flight Center (NASA-GSFC); 49(tl) NASA Jet Propulsion Laboratory (NASA-JPL); 60(cl) NASA-HQ-GRIN, (bc) NASA-JPL, (br) NASA-JPL; 65(br) NASA-JPL; 70–71(c) NASA-JPL; 71(tr) NASA Marshall Space Flight Center (NASA-MSFC), (bl) NASA-JPL, (br) NASA-JPL, (c) NASA-MSFC; 78(br) NASA-JPL; 79(cr) NASA-JPL; 75(tl) NASA-JPL Photolibrary.com 54–55 Steve Vidler Rex 63(cr) Nils Jorgensen Science Photo Library

46–47 J-P Metsavainio; 48–49 Chris Cook; 52(bl) Royal Astronomical Society; 53(tl) Detlev Van Ravenswaay; 54(tr) Eckhard Slawik; 56(bc) Dr Jeremy Burgess, (br) Royal Astronomical Society; 56–57(t) NYPL/Science Source; 57(cl); 58–59(tc); 60(tr) Richard J. Wainscoat, Peter Arnold inc.; 62–63(tc) J-P Metsavainio; 66 David Nunuk; 67(tr) Adam Hart-Davis; 68–69(b) Christian Darkin; 69(tr) Dr Jean Lorre; 72–73 Peter Menzel; 73(br) NRAO/AUI/NSF; 75(br) NASA, (cr) NASA/ESA/STSCI/R.Williams, (tl) NASA/WMAP Science Team, 76–77(bl) Mark Garlick, HDF-S Team; 80–81 Frank Zullo; 81(tl) Detlev Van Ravenswaay, (tr) Tony & Daphne Hallas; 82(r) NASA/Regina Mitchell-Ryall, Tom Farrar; 83(tr) European Space Agency, (cr) European Space Observatory; 87(b) JPL-Caltech; 91(bl); 92(c) JPL-Caltech, (t) NASA Langley Research Center (NASA-LaRC); 92–93(b); 96(bl); 96–97(t) Johns Hopkins University Applied Physics Laboratory/Southwest Research Institute; 98(c) JPL/University of Arizona; 98–99 oval insets JPL; 100(c); 101 Saturn JPL, Comet Borrelly JPL, Uranus, Neptune, Voyager 2 gold disk, Deep Space 1; 102(bl) STEREO; 103; 105(bl), (br); 108(bl) JPL/ Cornell; 110–111(bg) JPL/Cornell; 110(bl) Mariner 9 JPL, Mars 3 Scientific Visualization Studio, Mariner 4 JPL, Viking lander, Mars Global Russian Space Research Institute (IKI), Spirit/Opportunity rover JPL, Mars Surveyor; 111 Sojourner JPL; 112–113(bg); 117(br); 119(c), (b); Reconnaissance Orbiter JPL-Caltech, 119(t) NASA/JPL 122(bl) Johns Hopkins University Applied Physics Laboratory/Southwest Research Institute; 123(br); 124–125(bg) JPL-Caltech/T. Pyle (SSC)
Reuters 87(t) Kimimasa Mayama
Rex Features 105(tl); 113(br) NASA; 124(tl) Everett Collection, (c) c.Paramount/Everett; 125(b) KeystoneUSA-ZUMA
Science Photo Library 17(m) Mark Garlick, 24–25(m) Mark Garlick; 60(tr) Richard J. Wainscoat; 97(r) David Parker; 105(tr) NASA; 89(b) NASA; 94–95 David Ducros; 108–109(c), 111(tr) NASA/JPL/UA/Lockheed Martin, (b) NASA/JPL-Caltech, (tl) NASA; 116 Chris Butler 84–85 European Space Agency; 106 Detlev Van Ravenswaay; 115(tl) NASA/JPL/UA/Lockheed Martin; 114(t) SOHO/ ESA/NASA; 115(tl) NASA; 116 Chris Butler (Milky Way, Action Sports Photography (meteorite crater), Manamana (radio telescopes), Thomas **Shutterstock.com** back cover John A Davis
Nord (lunar eclipse), My Life Graphic (meteor shower), Triff (Sun); 1(c) Alexy Repka; 1(cr) Vadim Sadovski; 2–3 Denis Tabler; 4–5 Karin Wassmer; 9(bl) Dimec; 12(bl) tororo reaction; 22 MarcelClemens; 23(b) Action Sports Photography; 28(m) John A Davis; Eky Studio, (br) Karin Wassmer; 44(cr) Elisei Shafer, (cr) Thomas Barrat, (br) javarman; 49(tr) martiinllfluidworkshop; 50(cl) caesart; 50(br) Gordon Galbraith; 55(cr) Alex Hubenov; 60(tl frame) RDTMOR; 61(l) jordache; 63(bg) Vlue; 67(b) H. Damke; 75(tr) Dmitry Nikolajchuk; 86–87(c) pio3; 88–89(bg) Phase4Photography; 90–91(bg) SURABKY; 97(l) jamie cross; 96–97(bg) plavusa87; 100–101(bg) plavusa87

All other photographs are from:
DigitalSTOCK, digitalvision, John Foxx, PhotoAlto, PhotoDisc, PhotoEssentials, PhotoPro, Stockbyte

Every effort has been made to acknowledge the source and copyright holder of each picture. Miles Kelly Publishing apologizes for any unintentional errors or omissions.